Deschutes
Public Library

D0712305

DISCOVERING U.S. HISTORY

The Gilded Age and Progressivism

1891–1913

DISCOVERING U.S. HISTORY

The New World: Prehistory–1542

Colonial America: 1543–1763

Revolutionary America: 1764–1789

Early National America: 1790–1850

The Civil War Era: 1851–1865

The New South and the Old West: 1866–1890

The Gilded Age and Progressivism: 1891–1913

World War I and the Roaring Twenties: 1914–1928

The Great Depression: 1929–1938

World War II: 1939–1945

The Cold War and Postwar America: 1946–1963

Modern America: 1964–Present

C1

DISCOVERING U.S. HISTORY

The Gilded Age and Progressivism 1891–1913

Tim McNeese

Consulting Editor: Richard Jensen Ph.D.

CHELSEA HOUSE PUBLISHERS
An imprint of Infobase Publishing

THE GILDED AGE AND PROGRESSIVISM: 1891–1913

Copyright © 2010 Infobase Publishing

All rights reserved. No part of this book may be reproduced or utilized in any form or by any means, electronic or mechanical, including photocopying, recording, or by any information storage or retrieval systems, without permission in writing from the publisher. For information contact:

Chelsea House
An imprint of Infobase Publishing
132 West 31st Street
New York NY 10001

Library of Congress Cataloging-in-Publication Data
McNeese, Tim.
 The Gilded Age and Progressivism, 1891–1913 / by Tim McNeese.
   p. cm. — (Discovering U.S. history)
 Includes bibliographical references and index.
 ISBN 978-1-60413-355-4 (hardcover)
 1. United States—History—1865–1921—Juvenile literature. 2. United States—Social conditions—1865–1918—Juvenile literature. I. Title. II. Series.

 E661.M434 2009
 973.8—dc22

                  2009015012

Chelsea House books are available at special discounts when purchased in bulk quantities for businesses, associations, institutions, or sales promotions. Please call our Special Sales Department in New York at (212) 967-8800 or (800) 322-8755.

You can find Chelsea House on the World Wide Web at http://www.chelseahouse.com

The Discovering U.S. History series was produced for Chelsea House by Bender Richardson White, Uxbridge, UK

Editors: Lionel Bender and Susan Malyan
Designer and Picture Researcher: Ben White
Production: Kim Richardson
Maps and graphics: Stefan Chabluk
Cover design: Alicia Post

Cover printed by Bang Printing, Brainerd, MN
Book printed and bound by Bang Printing, Brainerd, MN
Date printed: April 2010
Printed in the United States of America

10 9 8 7 6 5 4 3 2 1

This book is printed on acid-free paper.

All links and web addresses were checked and verified to be correct at the time of publication. Because of the dynamic nature of the web, some addresses and links may have changed since publication and may no longer be valid.

Contents

Introduction

The Battleship Maine

When the battleship USS *Maine* sailed into Havana Harbor on the morning of January 25, 1898, Charles D. Sigsbee, the ship's captain, notes historian Michael Blow, sent a relieved telegram to his naval superiors in Washington, D.C., that they "had quietly arrived, 11 A.M. today; no demonstrations so far." Captain Sigsbee was certainly aware that he and his crew of 360 sailors and their officers had sailed into a potentially dangerous situation.

Although the arrival of the *Maine* was officially referred to by the U.S. Navy as a "goodwill" visit to the Spanish colonial island of Cuba, the very presence of the battleship at the island's largest port could only emphasize the underlying tensions between the United States and Spain, which were by then as thick as the tropical air. Colonial Cuba's 30-year, on-again-off-again rebellion against Spain, its European master for nearly four centuries, was again coming to a head. Riots were raging in the capital city of Havana, and the United

States government was on a mission to protect its interests on the Caribbean island.

AN ISLAND OF INTEREST

Cuba had long been a place of interest to the United States. Its location, situated only 70 miles (113 kilometers) south of Florida, was key, and through the nineteenth century some Americans had considered the island's potential as a possible U.S. territory. Over the years U.S. businessmen had become involved in Cuba's lucrative sugar industry. Various presidents—James K. Polk, Franklin Pierce, James Buchanan—had suggested the U.S. purchase Cuba from the Spaniards, but each attempt had been duly rebuffed by the Spanish government.

Then, after hundreds of years of colonial control, European colonies in the Caribbean started to seek independence. In 1868 the Cuban people, rich and poor, black and white, frustrated in their efforts, started a revolution. During the Ten Years' War that followed more than 50 Americans were killed while attempting to smuggle guns to the Cuban rebels. An outraged American public led President Ulysses S. Grant to call for U.S. naval action, but America's post-Civil War military was small and ineffective. Spain apologized, indemnities were paid to the families of the executed gunrunners, and the crisis passed.

THE CUBAN REVOLUTION

By 1878 Spanish officials had finally crushed their Cuban revolutionaries through a show of force and by promising them reforms. However, those reforms never came. Then, in 1895, Jose Marti, a Cuban poet and revolutionary, fomented another revolt against the Spanish through his Cuban Revolutionary Party, and the struggle for Cuban independence was on once again.

The rebels, called *insurectos*, targeted the island's sugar industry, hoping to bring the Spanish colonial power to its knees through economic chaos. This new revolt immediately drew the attention of the U.S. public. There were U.S. business investments at stake all over Cuba and at that time the United States was in the midst of a serious economic depression, but the most inspiring aspect of the revolution was the call by Cuban rebels for independence. For some in the United States, the Cuban fight reminded them of America's earlier struggle against British tyranny.

Despite the public's interest in the Cuban Revolution, the U.S. government was not prepared to become entangled in a fight between the Cubans and the Spanish. President Grover Cleveland announced official neutrality concerning the Cuban insurrection. Laws were enacted making it illegal for Americans to support the revolution, arm Cubans, or fight in the Cuban guerrilla forces. U.S. naval vessels patrolled the waters between Cuba and Florida, looking for U.S. gunrunners.

Yet Cleveland's policy was soon challenged by Congressmen on Capitol Hill. In 1896 the Senate passed a resolution of support for the revolution that recognized the right of the Cuban people to rebel against their Spanish colonial masters. House members rewrote the bill so that it now called for direct U.S. involvement in the revolution. By November 1896 officers at the Naval War College had worked up a plan that included U.S. military action in Cuba, as well as other Spanish colonies, such as Puerto Rico and the Philippines.

Public Support Grows

Yet, over the following 18 months, no overt military action was taken against the Spanish in support of Cuba. Through those months many sympathetic Americans read stories in their hometown newspapers about Spanish atrocities perpetrated against the Cuban people. Such articles were filled with sensational details, designed to solicit U.S. sympathy for Cuba. General Valeriano Weyler became, for many Americans, a household name. Weyler was a Spanish military commander whose ruthless campaign to rout out Cuban *insurectos* raised anger in the hearts of many Americans. Reports told of Weyler ferreting out revolutionaries from their jungle hide-outs. Those revolutionaries were then placed in concentration camps around Cuba by the hundreds of thousands, where many died of starvation and disease. Cuban homes, even whole villages, were allegedly burned by Weyler's men, and thousands of innocent islanders were killed. The U.S. press was soon referring to Weyler as "The Butcher." Laws or no laws, an increasing number of Americans were becoming everything but neutral toward the Cuban Revolution.

SLOW TO SUPPORT

But even as ordinary Americans were increasing their support for Cuba, the U.S. government remained behind the national curve. In November 1896, the country was in the midst of a presidential election, yet the candidates rarely referred to Cuba and the revolution at all. Republican William McKinley made no direct mention of Cuba in any campaign address, and, after he was elected, delivered his Inaugural Address with only an allusion to Cuba, stating: "War should never be entered upon until every agency of peace has failed; peace is preferable to war in almost every contingency."

Despite the president's words, during his first meeting with his new cabinet, McKinley received a recommendation from his consul general in Cuba, America's man in Havana, Fitzhugh Lee. (Lee's uncle had been the famous Confederate general, Robert E. Lee.) Lee suggested that a warship should be dispatched to Cuba as a show of force and to demonstrate to the Cubans the support of the U.S. government. At that meeting, McKinley, having just taken the office of president, denied Lee's request. Even then the Republican leader knew that he and his administration would eventually have to take steps that might involve the United States in the Cuban Revolution. The hue and cry of the American public was getting louder every day.

Over the next year, the rebellion in Cuba continued on and Americans watched anxiously. In the meantime, an assassination in Spain brought to power a new prime minister, Praxedes Mateo Sagasta, who was highly concerned over events in Cuba. Sagasta began pushing for autonomy for the island. By October 1897, new hope sprang when a new Spanish ruler in Cuba, General Ramon Blanco y Erenas, sent General Weyler packing back to Spain and promised the Cubans home rule, which meant they could govern themselves. But the rebels wanted more. They chose to continue their struggle, willing to accept nothing short of complete independence from Spain. *Cuba Libre!* (Free Cuba!) remained the rallying cry of the island's revolutionaries. While this was going on, many of the Spaniards in Cuba opposed Sagasta's policies of autonomy for their island. Military officials, government bureaucrats, and Spanish businessmen tried to block Sagasta at every turn.

THE *MAINE* SAILS SOUTH

Just two days after Sagasta came to power in Madrid, the U.S. secretary of the Navy, John D. Long, sent orders to the captain of the USS *Maine* to sail out of Chesapeake Bay, where the ship was engaged in maneuvers, and steam south. The *Maine* was one of the U.S. Navy's newest vessels, and a model for ships of the immediate future. When Congress had authorized its construction in 1886, the designers were handed a budget of $2.5 million to create a unique U.S. naval ship. The new vessel was designed to extend longer than a football field. It was double-hulled, steel constructed, and

The USS *Maine* steams into Havana Harbor, Cuba, on January 25, 1898. The crew of 355 men were apprehensive about entering Spanish-controlled waters—with good cause.

plated with a 12-inch (30-centimeter) thick band of nickel-steel armor, allowing the ship to withstand direct hits from an enemy warship with minimum damage.

Despite its size and weight, the *Maine* was built with the capacity to cut through the choppy waters of the Atlantic at a speed of 16 nautical miles per hour. The deck of the ship bristled with artillery, including four 10-in (25-cm) guns, two each built into a pair of separate turrets. The turrets were capable of turning the guns in a 180-degree arc, which allowed them to be fired from both sides of the ship. In addition, six 6-in (15-cm) guns were placed on the deck, two located in the bow, two in the stern, and two at mid-ships, while a second battery of seven six-pounder (2.7-kilogram) rapid-fire rifles were positioned by pairs in the bow and forward mid-ships, and three in the stern. There were eight one-pounder (0.5-kg) rapid-fire guns and four Gatling guns.

Below decks, the *Maine* was fitted with four torpedo tubes, two on each side of the ship, capable of firing White-head torpedoes. When finished, the *Maine* was an impressive sight, measuring a total of 324 feet (99 m) in length and 57 ft (17 m) wide and weighing 12 million lbs (5 million kg). The *Maine* was nothing short of naval innovation on the water.

Events Accelerate

By December 15, 1897, the *Maine* had arrived at Key West, less than 100 miles (160 km) from Havana. Just over a week earlier President McKinley, speaking to Congress, had admonished the Spanish to concentrate their efforts on political reform in Cuba. Soon events began to accelerate. Riots broke out in Havana on January 12, 1898. Less than a week later McKinley took a decisive step. He ordered the *Maine* to Cuba.

A few days later, on January 25, Captain Sigsbee delivered his ship to the island. That morning the U.S. vessel approached the narrow channel leading into Havana Harbor and sailed past Spanish shore batteries, where Spanish officials watched discreetly as the *Maine* progressed. Everyone onboard had been wary, uncertain what lay ahead. No U.S. warship had entered those waters in three years. Every man on deck had a loaded gun within reach, expecting action. Gunners had even taken their places on the turrets of the ship's 10-in (25-cm) guns, though observers on shore would not have been able to see them. As a handful of sailors watched from their vantage point on the deck, one turned to his shipmates and gave an ominous prediction, noted by historian Thomas Cutler: "We'll never get out of here alive."

AN UNCOMFORTABLE WAIT

The *Maine* was allowed into the harbor and piloted to her berth at buoy number 4, 400 yards (365 m) from the main wharf. Just 200 yds (180 m) to starboard sat the Spanish naval cruiser, *Alfonso XII*. On the U.S. vessel's opposite side was another Spanish ship, a transport called the *Legazpi*. Over the next three weeks, Captain Sigsbee ordered his men to remain on the ship. Only officers were allowed into Havana. Naval officials knew that just a few drunken American sailors getting in a fight with the local Spanish authorities could lead to an international incident.

As the days passed, life onboard the *Maine* became more and more unpleasant for the crew. Officers from the ship visited the *Alfonso XII* and Spanish officers came onboard the *Maine*—both were uneasy courtesy calls. The tension onboard the U.S. ship remained constant. "Why are we here?" some of the crew asked their superior officers. The harbor was polluted and smelly, giving off a foul odor from raw sewage. Circulars were tacked up along some Havana streets, threatening death to the Americans. Meanwhile rumors circulated that the harbor was littered with mines and underwater torpedoes, placed there by the Spanish. The Cuban nights were hot and humid, and everyone on the *Maine* seemed uncomfortable, as if they were waiting for something to happen.

Then on the evening of February 15, history caught up with the men onboard the USS *Maine*. At 9:40 P.M. Captain Sigsbee heard, as historian Terry Bilhartz notes: "a bursting, rending, and crashing roar of immense volume, largely metallic in character. It was followed by heavy, ominous metallic sounds. There was a trembling and lurching motion of the vessel, a list to port." Almost immediately, the electric lights in the quarters went out, and smoke drifted into the captain's cabin.

Uninjured, but certain that his ship had just experienced an explosion, the captain groped his way out of the dark cabin and followed the passageway that led to the ship's main deck. In the corridor, notes historian Blow, Sigsbee found his orderly, Private William Anthony, who said urgently: "Sir, I have to inform you that the ship has been blown up and is sinking."

In the dark, the explosions just seconds past, the captain of the *Maine* could only imagine what was taking place around him. Had his vessel been attacked? Had the Spanish finally had enough of the insult of a U.S. warship in Havana Harbor's waters? Would he, his men, his country finally be embroiled in a war for which so many of his countrymen had for so long clamored?

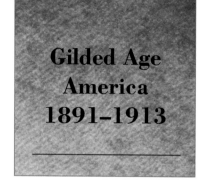

Gilded Age America 1891–1913

By 1913 there were 48 states —only Alaska and Hawaii were not yet part of the nation. Most of the major cities were well established and had become populated by large numbers of immigrants from many different countries. By this time too, all Native Americans had been resettled on reservations.

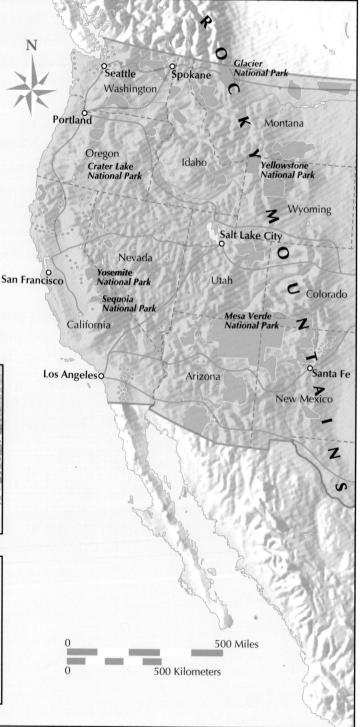

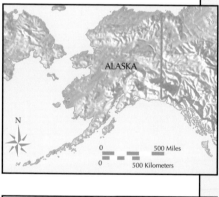

North Dakota

Minnesota

St. Paul

Minneapolis

South Dakota

Custer

Wounded Knee

Nebraska

Omaha

Wisconsin

Michigan

Milwaukee

Chicago

Iowa

Illinois

Indiana

Rochester

Buffalo

Detroit

Cleveland

Pittsburgh

Ohio

West Virginia

New York

Adams

Seneca Falls

Maine

Vermont

New Hampshire

Massachusetts

Boston

Rhode Island

Connecticut

Pennsylvania

Philadelphia

New York City

New Jersey

Washington D.C.

Delaware

Maryland

Virginia

Richmond

APPALACHIAN MOUNTAINS

Kansas City

Kansas

St. Louis

Missouri

Kentucky

Tennessee

North Carolina

South Carolina

Guthrie

Oklahoma

Arkansas

Birmingham

Atlanta

Tuskegee

Alabama

Georgia

Fort Worth

Dallas

Louisiana

Texas

Mississippi

Jacksonville

New Orleans

Florida

Houston

San Antonio

Modern border of the U.S.A.

Native American Reservations

National Parks

Railroad

17

1

The Rise of the Modern City

The America of the last decade of the nineteenth century was in the midst of growing pains. For more than a century the United States had developed as a country constantly bursting at the seams, always in motion, endlessly in search of new horizons. Throughout the 1800s Americans had moved West by the hundreds of thousands, their numbers including restless easterners, newly arrived European immigrants, and newly freed slaves. The advance of the American republic had delivered people to nearly every remote corner of the nation.

Aiding this expansion was an ever-changing series of technological advances, tapping everything from water power to steam, and electricity to gasoline. Inventions including steamboats, railroads, subways, and early automobiles conquered distances by reducing travel times. The invention of the airplane (1903) just missed flying in the nineteenth century by three years. Innovative American tinkerers, mechanics, machinists, and forward-thinking chemists transformed life in the United States. All this occurred during a century in which little remained static. Change was everywhere; it was a symbol of the greatness of the American system, of patriotic pride.

Perhaps, though, the decade of the greatest change was the century's last. The 1890s would come to represent years of great leaps forward, a transitional time connecting the past with the approaching, perhaps intimidating future of the twentieth century. By the turn of the century America had come of age, having conquered its last frontiers and made the transition from a largely rural nation of yeoman farmers to an industrial giant, whose reach for markets overseas knew no bounds. The country had also become increasingly urbanized, as millions of Americans, as well as new immigrant arrivals, created cities of scope, where new technologies allowed Americans to build, not just toward the next horizon, but toward the sky.

URBAN AMERICA

The transition from a rural America to an urbanized one did not take place overnight. Throughout the nineteenth century cities were filling up, it seemed, to the point of capacity. In New York the influential newspaper editor, Horace Greeley, commented that his fellow New Yorkers, who then numbered well over 1 million, were living cheek-to-jowl, crowded together in neighborhoods and boroughs with new numbers arriving daily. Historian Lawrence Salinger notes Greeley's observation: "We cannot all live in cities," he admonished in print, "yet nearly all seem determined to do so." But Greeley was writing about the U.S. cities of the late 1860s, not the 1890s.

In the half-century between 1860 and 1910 the nation's city dwellers increased from 6 million to 44 million. The last three decades of the nineteenth century saw tremendous growth in America's urban populations. As early as 1870 approximately a dozen U.S. cities were home to at least 100,000 residents each. The numbers tell the story. Between 1870 and 1900 the northern city of Detroit grew from 80,000 to 285,000 inhabitants, while the southern city of Atlanta mushroomed from 22,000 to 90,000. Philadelphia, established in the late 1600s, doubled its population during the last three decades of the century, from 675,000 to over 1.3 million.

Such growth was not limited to America's older, eastern urban communities. Out on the prairies of Illinois, Chicago reached 1.7 million people, even after much of the city had been destroyed by a devastating fire in 1871. On the West Coast, Los Angeles was a frontier town of fewer than 6,000 people in 1870, but had reached 100,000 by the turn of the century. But the leader of the urbanized pack was New York City. Its population reached a whopping 3.4 million by 1900, after the consolidation of its five boroughs in 1898.

In 1860, 80 percent of Americans lived in places with fewer than 2,500 local residents. By 1900 one out of every seven Americans called home a city of more than a quarter million people. That same year one U.S. resident in twelve lived either in New York, Philadelphia, or Chicago. It all represented one of the greatest demographic shifts in U.S. history to that date.

Perhaps Chicago was the greatest of the urban miracles of the last 30 years of the nineteenth century. Originally a fort on the colonial frontier, Chicago grew by leaps and bounds following the opening of the Erie Canal in 1825. By the time of the Civil War, Chicago, notes historian Bernard Weisberger, "saw hundreds of lake vessels swarming in and out of its wharves in a year, loaded with millions of bushels of flour and grain, and hundreds of millions of board feet of lumber." In the midst of all that bustle, fire swept through the city in 1871, destroying block after block. But razed Chicago was soon a raised Chicago, as local residents built again on top of its ruins, and the city's population reached 1 million within 20 years. Some of the nation's most innovative architects seized the opportunity to rebuild the city using their building designs.

CITIES IN TRANSFORMATION

America's cities were not simply changing in population numbers during these final decades of the nineteenth century. The country's earlier urban centers had sprung up in the days prior to mass transportation and had been "walking cities," where the vast majority of the residents had to walk from their houses or apartments to their places of work. These earlier communities had been small in landmass, compact, and densely populated, often covering an area with a radius of just 2 miles (3 km) from the center of town. This distance could be covered on foot by most city dwellers in 30 minutes. Even the largest of the nation's cities, including New York and Philadelphia, fit that earlier model.

Everyone and everything was piled on top of each other. With few city codes or building regulations, cities of the early 1800s stacked neighborhoods with homes, storefronts, factories, schools, and churches. The poor and the rich might even live nearly side by side, the wealthiest living close to the heart of the city, with poorer neighborhoods literally just around the corner. People came and went on a social, even personal, basis with almost no segregation by race or social status. Rich men walked the streets with poor immigrants, even as blacks and whites worked side by side. U.S. cities had not reached their later levels of impersonal urban living.

This urban social structure was brought down by the advances of industrialization. As factories and other industrial plants were built near already existing cities, those cityscapes spread out to connect the two. U.S. city growth during the last decades of the nineteenth century is paralleled by industrial development. Cities became immense, their streets stretching on seemingly without end. Suddenly urban dwellers could not possibly be familiar with the entire city they called home. They knew only their portion, their borough, the ward in which they voted. The age of the modern city had arrived.

TECHNOLOGY AND URBAN DEVELOPMENT

As cities grew, new technologies were needed to accommodate the scope of urban life. Hundreds of thousands of people needed mobility—the means to get to and from the furthest ends of their city for work, social contacts, shopping, and leisure. Mass transportation systems were crucial.

In 1870 New York saw its first elevated railway system, built to take the pressure off the crushing street traffic. The line followed Ninth Avenue for several miles and later sections were added along Second, Third, and Sixth Avenues. Above the streets, steam trains pulled passenger cars, as sparks, cinders, and dripping oil fell on unsuspecting pedestrians. Historian Robert G. Athearn notes that "the El" was "steam-driven, noisy, and a ghastly fire hazard, but it was worshiped as progress and imitated." New York introduced other technological innovations throughout the decade, including early telephones in 1877 and harshly brilliant arc lights along city streets in 1880.

In the spring of 1883 the Brooklyn Bridge—the world's longest suspension bridge—opened to connect Manhattan with Brooklyn, then still a separate city. The city's growing population demanded more bridges, leading to the Washington Bridge across the Harlem River in 1889. A third bridge went under construction in 1896. With the city teeming with people, the need for water also became crucial, leading to the construction between 1885 and 1892 of tunnels extending north to tap the Croton Watershed. This new water system delivered 300 million gallons (1,360 million liters) of water to New York City daily, but it was soon inadequate. Within 20 years the water system for New York was extended even further north.

SKYSCRAPERS

New York grew out, up, and down. The 1890s introduced skyscrapers to the city, such as the Flatiron Building, which still stands more than a century later. Within the first decade of the twentieth century New York buildings reached skyward to 30 stories.

Skyscrapers represented a totally new way of building. Traditional brick-and-mortar or stone buildings could not be built higher than 10 stories, since the structure lacked adequate support for the increased weight. But, in 1885, a New York architect named William BeBaron Jenney created a new "skeleton" that allowed buildings to rise higher than ever. His idea was to use cast iron and steel as the frame of the building, covered over with light brick, stone, and other masonry. To that end, he designed the Home Insurance Building in Chicago, an early skyscraper that was only 10 stories tall, but included a steel skeleton and light masonry. Then an architectural associate of Jenney's, Louis Henri Sullivan, designed his own skyscrapers, including the 10-story Wainwright Building in St. Louis and the Transportation Building in Chicago, followed by his 13-story Guaranty Building (today known as the Prudential Building) in Buffalo in 1894. Sullivan's building credo was "form follows function," resulting in skyscrapers featuring straight exterior lines and an interior functionality.

The Flatiron Building in New York City, shown here under construction, was one of the earliest skyscrapers. Designed by architect Daniel Burnham, it was completed in 1902 and is 22 stories high.

Skyscrapers towered higher than any European cathedrals, their stone exteriors gleaming with the spit and polish of a new American era. The interiors of such buildings were as impressive as their newly designed exteriors, with the interconnected twin miracles of running water and indoor bathrooms, and all interiors lit up with electric lights.

Electricity was an old power newly harnessed in these cities. Humming electric elevators whisked visitors, businessmen, and tenants up 20 floors and higher. All along the city streets, a spider's web of electrical lines ran from pole to pole, carrying power from generators to buildings and lighting up the urban world. Even at night, the cities could show off, gleaming under the light of street lamps, where city dwellers could come and go long after the sun went down. Electricity was the power of the new U.S. urban landscapes. In Boston, at the old Bijou Theatre, theater patrons could enjoy evening performances with the introduction of a 650-bulb electrical light system. At the tricorner of New York's Fifth Avenue, Broadway, and 23rd Street, the street was illuminated by a 50-ft (15-m)-tall sign, with green lights forming the outline of a giant pickle, and rows of white lights spelling out the advertiser: "HEINZ, 57 Varieties."

The Bigger the Better

The new skyscrapers excited many Americans, even though some people feared what they might symbolize. In the January 21, 1906, Sunday edition of the *New York Times*, American writer Henry James referred disparagingly to the new vertical growth of New York, noting "the multitudinous skyscrapers standing up to the view... like extravagant pins in a cushion already overplanted, and stuck in as in the dark, anywhere and anyhow."

But most Americans saw the skyscrapers as mile markers of progress, visible signs of the expanding role of U.S.

commerce and business in world markets. The bigger the better. Even U.S. presidents made their contribution. Woodrow Wilson, in 1913, attended an opening ceremony for the newly constructed 792-ft (241-m)-tall Woolworth Building, then the largest building in the country. With fanfare, the president pressed a ceremonial button that lit up the entire building. The Woolworth Building, a Neo-Gothic monster rising 57 stories above New York City, is still counted among the 50 tallest buildings in the world.

SUBWAYS AND SLUMS

By the turn of the century, New York City's first subway was under construction, a system of 13 miles (21 km) of subterranean tunnels and 3 miles (5 km) of elevated track. Although only a few miles in length, this first New York City subway proved to be the beginning of a project that would continue for the next 40 years and would extend for hundreds of miles beneath the city streets. By design, the subway was intended to carry approximately 600,000 passengers daily, but the number of riders topped that figure by October 1905. The number continued to rise, reaching 800,000 daily passengers by early 1908. Additional miles of subway were quickly added.

Not all of New York's growth was enviable. While great skyscrapers went up and subways snaked under the city's streets, some New York neighborhoods were dirty, crowded, unsanitary places to live. In 1900 the New York State Tenement House Commission reported that, just in Manhattan, more than 1 million residents were stuffed into 43,000 inferior tenement houses. The report observed, notes historian Bernard Weisberger, that "adequate light and air, perfect sanitation, even passable home environment" was not available in those tenement buildings. Slums were not new to New York; there were just more and more city blocks of them.

TENEMENTS

Many early tenements had windows opening into interior hallways and so were dark and poorly ventilated. In 1901 New York State passed an act that required tenements to have an open courtyard, indoor toilets, fire escapes, and an outward facing window in every room. In practice, many of these windows opened into light wells.

Labels for one tenement
1. Fire escape
2. Living room
3. Kitchen
4. Bedroom 1
5. Bedroom 2
6. Bathroom
7. Hallway
8. Cut away showing light well
9. Washing line

PEOPLE MOVERS

Other U.S. cities were not without their innovative contributions to twentieth-century urban progress. Almost 3,000 miles (4,800 km) from New York, cable cars were introduced to San Francisco's streets in 1873. Back East, hilly Pittsburgh introduced its first cable cars during the 1870s, as well. While horse-drawn streetcars, called omnibuses, had been a common sight in the nation's cities throughout the 1800s, the first commercially viable electric streetcars went on line in Richmond, Virginia, in 1888. A singular innovation made this type of transportation system possible. That year a former naval engineer, Frank Sprague, created the system by stringing overhead wires that produced an electrical current. The result was the introduction of electrified trolleys that could move along city streets at speeds of between 10 and 12 miles per hour (16 to 19 kmph), with some even reaching speeds of 20 mph (32 kmph).

The technology caught on immediately. By the turn of the century there were 30,000 trolley cars in use in the United States, rolling along 15,000 miles (24,000 km) of track. By 1902, 97 percent of urban trolley lines had been electrified. Such lines connected sprawling suburbs to the urban centers, and even connected cities themselves, such as a trolley line between New York and Boston, which opened in 1920. The electric trolley became, notes historian James Kirby Martin, "one of the most rapidly accepted innovations in the history of technology." A British visitor to one U.S. metropolis observed, notes historian Sam Halper: "The thoroughfares are crowded, busy and bustling; and abounding signs of life and energy in the people are everywhere apparent."

Trolley systems, plus the handful of subway systems around the country, meant that urban workers could now live as far as 5 miles (8 km) from their work place and still travel there in less than an hour. By the early 1890s such railways were commonplace, amounting to 10,000 miles (16,000 km) of track in cities across the country. The late 1870s saw public waterworks in 600 U.S. cities, and thousands of such systems over the following generation. There were new sewer systems and garbage collecting systems in place, which helped to reduce the threat of epidemic diseases, such as typhoid and cholera.

NEW ARRIVALS

U.S. cities became meccas. Many people who moved to these urban centers during the last decades of the nineteenth century were from rural areas. Farm girls, for example, who had

RESTRICTIONS ON IMMIGRATION

As millions of immigrants poured into the United States during the late nineteenth century, some government officials sought to block some people from entering the country. In 1891 a House member from Massachusetts, Henry Cabot Lodge, tried to exclude people who could not read or write. Had this test been implemented, many would-be immigrants would have been turned away.

Throughout more than a quarter century of trying, Lodge's and similar bills were always vetoed by Presidents Cleveland, Taft, and Wilson. Finally, Congress overrode Wilson's objections in 1917.

But European populations were not the most restricted immigrant groups wanting to enter America. Perhaps no group was more restricted than the Chinese.

In 1880 California was home to 75,000 Chinese immigrants, making up about 11 percent of the state's population. Many of them had made valuable contributions to the building of the western railroads. As their numbers increased, however, some whites started to resent them. They were driven by their own racism and by a belief that Chinese workers drove down wages because they would work for less.

no prospects of owning the family farm and faced few job opportunities, often moved to the cities, where they found employment as secretaries, stenographers, store clerks, seamstresses, and telephone operators.

Many others who found their way to the U.S. cities were not native-born Americans but immigrants, who came to the United States before and after 1900. They reached U.S. shores by the millions, often traveling in the cramped "steerage" compartments of great passenger ships. During the 1880s approximately 5 million foreigners immigrated to the United States. Many were drawn to America as a land of opportunity.

The year 1880, then, began to witness restrictions on Chinese immigrants. First the government signed a treaty with China allowing the U.S. to regulate or limit the number of immigrants allowed in from China. In 1882 Congress passed a bill suspending the entry of Chinese immigrants to the States. The Chinese Exclusion Act was renewed periodically and barriers continued against the Chinese until 1943.

Since Chinese immigration continued through the latter decades of the nineteenth and early twentieth centuries, even if it was only a trickle of people, an immigrant point of entry was necessary in California. The Ellis Island alternative was the Immigration Station on Angel Island, located about 6 miles (10 km) offshore from San Francisco. It opened in 1910 as a processing station for Asian immigrants, many of them from China.

There were restrictions on those seeking entrance into the United States. Those who had a Chinese-American parent were typically allowed in, as well as those who were students, teachers, or merchants. The process of admission might be stretched out for weeks or months, and 30 percent of Chinese applicants were turned away, compared to just 2 percent of the Europeans who were processed during these same decades at Ellis Island.

The tide began to rise just after the Civil War, from under 3 million immigrants during the 1870s to more than 5 million by the following decade. The 1890s, which included several years of U.S. economic depression, saw a drop to just over 3.5 million. Then, the wave crested, with nearly 9 million newcomers entering the United States during the first decade of the twentieth century. Earlier years, including the period before the Civil War, had seen the coming of mostly western Europeans—Germans, Scandinavians, French, and boatloads of Irish. But by the 1870s many were coming from eastern and southern Europe, including Poles, Czechs, Slovaks, Serbs, Croats, Italians, Romanians, Greeks, Hungarians, and Russian Jews. They brought with them their unique languages, cultural practices, and different religions, including Catholicism, Judaism, and Orthodox faiths.

POINT OF ENTRY

People arriving in the United States from Europe needed to be processed for entry into the country. The most common port of arrival was New York. In 1890 the federal government set up a new Bureau of Immigration to handle the admission of foreign arrivals. Congress voted monies for the construction of a new receiving center on a small island off the coast of New Jersey, just a quarter mile (half kilometer) from the Statue of Liberty, which the French government had sent as a gift to the United States in 1886. Called Ellis Island, the facility opened its doors in 1892, and continued as the conduit for processing many of the immigrants who arrived in New York until 1954.

The original Ellis Island Immigration Station was a 400-foot (122-m)-long building, fashioned out of Georgia pine and resembling a barn. That building burned after just five years, and was replaced by a giant 220,000-square-ft (20,000-sq-m), red brick structure, topped with four large copper-plated domes, giving the appearance of a European state building or palace.

Here, immigrants were herded through a system that was more interested in weeding out undesirables than in welcoming foreigners to America's shores. Arrivals were given

Newly landed European immigrants wait on the dock at Ellis Island in about 1900. Immigrants were drawn to America by the dream of a better future, but life for many of them proved tough.

the once over by doctors, who examined them for communicable diseases. They were asked about their politics, job prospects, and U.S. connections. In many cases, "odd-sounding" foreign names were altered. Those who passed all the exams and questions were often given admittance in a few hours. But approximately 1 in every 50 people was not admitted and would be sent back, with the ship company paying all expenses for their return trip.

Approximately 12 million people were processed at Ellis Island. Today, two out of every five Americans are descended from someone who passed through Ellis Island. During the facility's busiest year, 1907, 500,000 foreigners were funneled along the immense, open Great Hall, at a pace of 5,000 people daily. However, not everyone who arrived by ship in New York was required to go through examination at Ellis. Those immigrants who had traveled in first- or second-class cabins were allowed to bypass the facility completely.

STARTING A NEW LIFE

Once they were admitted, the new arrivals were typically overjoyed to have made their way to America. Many were greeted by friends and family who had come over before them and who could help pave the way for the immigrant's new life in the United States. Some immigrants were recruited immediately to work for low wages in mines, mills, factories, and sweat shops in New York, or other U.S. cities, such as Buffalo, Pittsburgh, St. Louis, Cleveland, and Chicago. Many immigrants from such places as Poland, Hungary, Italy, as well as Slovaks and Bohemians, found jobs as miners. Steel mills hired Slavs and Poles—men who might be already accustomed to back-breaking labor. Textile mills hired Greeks. Russians and Polish Jews might be hired in the garment industries or in the pushcart trade. In nearly every case, these jobs paid poorly and the work was taxing.

For those who remained to work in the urban centers, their new homes might be only a basic tenement. During the last 20 or so years of the nineteenth century the cities became so crowded with immigrant workers that tenement buildings were constructed with more stories. They also had a new interior design, called a "dumbbell," since New York housing codes required a 2-ft (60-cm)-wide air shaft between two buildings, which gave the look of a dumbbell when viewed from above.

These buildings could house between 24 and 32 families per floor, which allowed tenement owners to stuff 4,000 people into a single city block. Such buildings were unsafe fire traps, poorly heated, hot in the summer, cold in the winter. Toilets for a building were located outside and typically overused, with only two toilets constructed per floor. Diseases spread like wild fire in such cramped buildings, and infant mortality rates sometimes were as high as 60 percent. Life for many new immigrants soon revealed an America where the streets were not exactly paved with gold.

Yet, for many immigrants from Europe life in the United States represented a world of greater opportunities for themselves and for their children. Wages might be low, but better than in their nation of origin. Children were provided with free education and enrolled in public schools, where they could become the first generation in their families to learn the English language, which helped the immigrant family assimilate into the mainstream of U.S. life.

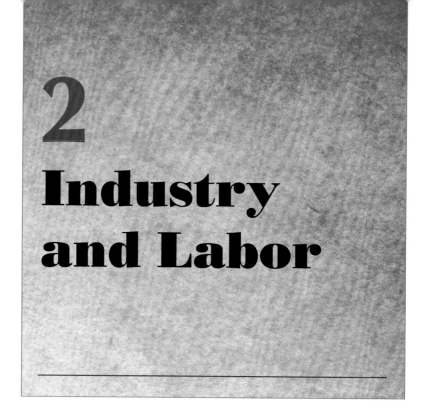

2

Industry and Labor

By the 1890s the United States had progressed from being a rural nation dotted by many thousands of small farms. It was now a country that represented, to other industrialized nations, a giant; a colossus powered by steam, electricity, and oil. The preceding decades were years in which farming remained important, with farm production doubling between 1870 and 1900. But the output of the manufacturing sector—the nation's mines, mills, factories, and other industrial plants—grew six fold during those same decades.

The American people experienced more change in one or two generations than their ancestors had in one or two centuries. The United States of 1900 was a highly mechanized nation, which ran on clocks and schedules, its production levels set by mass production and mass consumerism. The industrial revolution that had taken root in America during the late eighteenth and early nineteenth centuries had finally hit a great stride of production, output, and progress, even if much of the development of industry was done on the backs of an underpaid working class.

A NEW ERA OF TECHNOLOGY

During the latter decades of the nineteenth century U.S. technology was king. In 1876, during the nation's celebration of its 100th birthday, some of those technological advances were on display at the Centennial Exposition in Philadelphia. On the day the exposition opened, the emperor of Brazil was on hand to flip a great switch that started one of the largest steam engines in the world. Later that day he was introduced to a new invention, the telephone, just patented by Alexander Graham Bell. The emperor was astounded at the simple tabletop device. "It talks," he said in disbelief.

Thomas Edison

While Bell's discovery would have unlimited impact on the future, that same year saw the opening of the most productive invention laboratory in America—Thomas Alva Edison's creative beehive, located in Menlo Park, New Jersey. Surrounding himself with the best electrical scientists and mechanical tinkerers, Edison, then only in his late twenties, had already invented the mimeograph machine, the multiplex telegraph, and an electric stock ticker to allow brokers to keep an up-to-the-minute pulse of the nation's stock exchange. In October 1879 he and his team invented an artificial light, an incandescent bulb that burned for 13 hours. Within a couple of months Edison had strung up hundreds of such lights in his lab and invited thousands of people to come at night to see for themselves his new world of light. Edison, who was more than just an eccentric inventor, then went on to establish the Edison Electric Light Company, in 1882, to provide the power for electrifying the streets of New York. The darkness has been illuminated ever since.

While Edison was at the vanguard of the inventing class during the last decades of the nineteenth century and into the early twentieth, he was not alone. Through the 1870s, 13,000 patents were issued on average each year. During the 20 years following the end of the Civil War, American inventors took out nearly 500,000 patents.

The list of new American inventions seemed limitless: Edison's phonograph in 1877, the cash register in 1879, linotype in newspaper publishing in 1886, the Kodak camera in 1888. George Westinghouse, who invented the air brake for trains, also developed the first alternating current system for the transmission of electricity in 1886, which Edison used in developing his own electric company. Westinghouse produced much of the equipment used in such plants and he also created a viable electric motor which allowed for the use of electricity as a power source in factories. Innovations like these only proved the point made by a contemporary writer, notes historian John A. Kouwenhoven: "Our greatest thinkers are not in the library, nor the capitol, but in the machine shop."

AUTOMOBILES, AIRPLANES, AND RAILROADS

Transportation saw many innovations, including the development of the automobile. While the automobile was not an American invention, men such as Henry Ford were soon designing their own models, using internal combustion engines fueled with gasoline. By the turn of the century Henry Ford and other innovators like him were producing automobiles by the thousands. Three years later, a pair of brothers from Dayton, Ohio, working in the backroom of their bicycle shop, invented a successful heavier-than-aircraft—the first airplane. Orville and Wilbur Wright spent years getting their glider and engine craft to take to the air,

HENRY FORD AND THE MODEL T

The Ford Model T was the automobile that "put America on wheels"—an affordable car for the masses. Unlike earlier cars, which were hand-crafted, the Model T was produced using a new system—the assembly line. More than 15 million of them were sold between 1908 and 1927.

John D. Rockefeller's Standard Oil company was quick to cash in on the increased demand for gasoline.

Partly built cars moved along a conveyor in front of workers, who added new components. This method was so efficient that a Model T could be built in just 93 minutes.

and more years improving their first plane. They were insep-
arable until Wilbur died of typhoid fever in 1912.

But of all the transportation innovations of the late
nineteenth century, none had a greater impact on the U.S.
economy than the nation's railroad system. The first trans-
continental rail line was completed across the West in 1869.
The line represented such a massive building project that
it required two large-scale corporations to build it—the
Union Pacific and the Central Pacific Railroads. Other cross-
country lines followed over the next 20 years, including the
Southern Pacific, the Northern Pacific, and the Atchison,
Topeka, and Santa Fe. A fifth line, the Great Northern, was
completed in the early 1890s. These railroad companies represented the first giant businesses in America. Trains carried
everything from raw materials for manufacturing, to cattle,
to finished goods, to passengers.

MANUFACTURING GOODS

With the aid of the railroads, the U.S. manufacturing sector
took off like a rocket, experiencing unprecedented growth.
The level of production of capital goods, following the Civil
War, expanded at an average of 7 percent annually. By 1900
U.S. production plants churned out goods worth $13 bil-
lion, more than six times greater than in 1865. Through
those decades U.S. productivity moved up from fourth in
the world to number one.

Industry ran at a dizzying rate, mass-producing everything from shoes to cigarettes. These plants were switch-
ing from water power to steam power, produced by giant,
coal-fired boiler systems. Coal was also in use to heat up
the nation's open-hearth furnaces and iron and steel mills.
America's steel industry went through extraordinary expansion, surpassing all European producers, as mills blasted out
steel rails for the railroads and girders for the skyscrapers,

The conductor, crew, and dog mascot of a Central Pacific Railroad train pose by the locomotive during a station stop at Mill City, Nevada, in 1883. The line ran from Sacramento, California, to Ogden, Utah.

plus thousands of other products, including machine parts to build machines that could then produce other goods. America's industrial wheels were turning rapidly.

While earlier generations of Americans had produced many of the things they needed on their own, in their own homes—candles, tools, furniture, clothing, soap—industry was now beginning to mass produce all these items, and more. Machines were designed to produce thousands of a single item a day, under one roof, and providing labor for, perhaps, hundreds of people. Sometimes such machines brought significant change. In 1881, for example, a cigarette-making machine was invented that was capable of producing 7,000 cigarettes an hour. Previously, a single worker could only produce 3,000 cigarettes in an entire working day. At the new rate just 15 such machines were capable of producing the entire nation's cigarette needs. Importantly, with the mass production of inexpensive cigarettes, more and more smokers put away their pipes and turned to cigarettes, creating a national smoking habit where one had largely not existed before.

A WHOLE STORE OF GOODS

Much of the fuel behind the new expanding economy was a developing market for more manufactured goods. New means of marketing products came into practice, including the opening of mail-order businesses, following the Civil War. With railroads capable of delivering purchases almost anywhere in the country in a short time, plus low postal and freight costs, people even in remote areas of the country suddenly had a huge variety of goods available to them, inside the illustrated catalogs produced by the mail-order houses. Such businesses as Sears, Roebuck and Company and Montgomery Ward relied on selling at long distances, offering the latest variety of consumer goods. Separated only by a few pages of print was a whole store of goods—everything from Kodak box cameras to buggy whips, men's derbies to gang plows, lace hankies to patent medicines. The 1897 Sears catalog offered men's cashmere suits for $6, the Royal Grinder Wind Mill for $23, a half dozen solid sterling silver tea spoons for $3.45, and a Colt single action revolver for $12.95—something for everyone. Sears even made available by mail order food items normally found in local general stores, such as Aunt Jemima's Pancake Flour and Armour's summer sausage.

For those who lived in the urban centers, a new innovation called the chain store opened up for business. By the turn of the century five or six such chains were in operation around the country, including the Great Atlantic and Pacific Tea Company, the A&P. Frank and Charles Woolworth headed their famous "Woolworth's Five and Dime" store chain, which had 1,000 outlets by the end of World War I.

But the true meccas for urban shoppers were the department stores that paralleled the development of the chain stores. These stores offered a host of goods, all neatly "departmentalized" by product types. These were posh places, indeed, featuring richly carpeted floors, marble staircases, crystal chandeliers, and well-dressed clerks ready to serve the discerning customer. By 1900 everyone knew the names of the biggest department stores—Marshall Field in Chicago, Wanamaker's in Philadelphia, and Macy's in New York.

THE TYCOONS OF THE MARKET PLACE

While innovation and invention drove much of the new U.S. economy of the late nineteenth century, there were also enormously influential men of capital, the so-called "captains of industry." These entrepreneurs skillfully and sometimes ruthlessly organized giant corporations. Among the most significant of these hugely influential capitalists were John D. Rockefeller, Andrew Carnegie, and J. Pierpont Morgan.

Rockefeller: the Oil Magnate

John D. Rockefeller was a New Yorker, born to a pious Baptist mother and a less-than-disciplined father, who moved out to Ohio as a young man to get in on the fledgling oil business of the 1860s. In 1862 he formed a two-man partnership in an oil refinery. The business grew and, by 1870, Rockefeller pooled his interests together into a single corporation powerhouse—the Standard Oil Company of Ohio. He capitalized his new company with $1 million.

But, with so many smaller companies dealing in the oil boom of the period, it was difficult to make money, and the price of oil dropped due to extensive competition. Rockefeller decided to do something about those annoying competitors. In 1872 he formed the South Improvement Company, a large marketing firm for his oil. Soon, he was making sweetheart deals with local railroad companies, who gave him refunds (called rebates) on the standard freight rate to ship his oil, since he had so much to ship. Having cut freight costs, Rockefeller could undersell his competitors. He then began approaching those competitors to buy them out. By 1879 Rockefeller's Standard Oil Company was in control of more than 90 percent of oil refining in the United States.

Another business practice that helped ensure Rockefeller's success was that of "vertical integration." This meant that Rockefeller produced everything that he needed to operate in the oil business. Since he needed oil barrels and cans, he built a plant to make his own. He also built the pipelines that delivered his oil to the railroads, tank cars to carry oil by rail, and his own oil storage facilities. For Rockefeller, the practice made it possible for him to see to his business motto—"pay nobody a profit"—except himself.

This cartoon from 1884, entitled *Monster Monopoly*, depicts John D. Rockefeller's Standard Oil Company as a threatening, octopus-like creature, with its tentacles gripping everything from the railroad to banks, insurance companies, and shipping.

To keep all these various parts of the oil "pie" together in a seamless business entity, Rockefeller and his partners relied on a business structure that was legal at the time—the trust. In 1882 the 37 stockholders in Rockefeller's various oil-related businesses handed over their stock interests to nine trustees, receiving "trust certificates" instead. These trustees could then make the decisions concerning all of Standard's previously separated interests. Many other large-scale business entrepreneurs also came to rely on the trust structure. In the end, the trust nearly eliminated any real competition within a given business field.

In 1892 the government caught up with such business practices, as the U.S. Supreme Court ordered the Standard Oil Trust to be broken up. But Rockefeller simply dodged the court's decision, as well as the 1890 Sherman Antitrust Act, by creating another business structure called the interlocking directory. This allowed the boards of directors of different companies to be the same men, who then made decisions for all the parts of the system.

Carnegie: "The Gospel of Wealth"

Another entrepreneurial innovator in the world of corporate business was a Scottish immigrant, Andrew Carnegie. His father was a poor weaver who moved his family to the United States, and settled in Allegheny, Pennsylvania. Carnegie worked various low-paying jobs, starting at age 13 as a bobbin boy in a textile mile, where he earned $1.20 a week. By 14 he was a telegrapher making $2.50 weekly, eventually becoming the telegrapher and secretary to the superintendent of the Pennsylvania Railroad. In time, young Carnegie became the railroad's new superintendent.

In 1865 he struck out in business on his own, investing in iron making and bridge building. Steel seemed the metal of the future and in 1872, while on a business trip to the British

Isles, Carnegie met an Englishman named Henry Bessemer, who had created a method of mass-producing steel called the Bessemer Process. The process allowed for the production of steel at competitive prices. Carnegie returned to the States, inspired to build a steel-producing factory. He told a friend, notes historian Matthew Josephson, "The day of iron has passed! Steel is king!"

Other businessmen were also investing in their own steel plants at the time, but Carnegie moved to the front of the pack immediately. He was never an expert on steel making per se, but he was a great business organizer and promoter. He was adept at picking the talent he needed to run both the plants themselves and those who worked the office or business end of steel making. Carnegie put the latest equipment in his steel mills, spent money during times of recession, and kept his costs low.

Like Rockefeller, Carnegie relied on vertical integration, ultimately owning the mines, the railroads, the mills, and everything else needed to transform raw materials into steel and then get the steel to market. Carnegie steel was soon being used to build the Brooklyn Bridge, New York's elevated railway system, and the interior skeleton of the Washington Monument.

As Carnegie had predicted, steel really did become king. The new mass-production techniques soon resulted in huge increases in steel production. In 1870, the country's foundries and mills produced a total of 850,000 tons (771,000 tonnes) of steel. By 1900, steel production had mushroomed to more than 10.5 million t (9.5 million T) and was still growing at a considerable pace. The manufacture of steel required coal for energy, so increases in coal production paralleled steel's advance. American miners extracted 500,000 t (454,000 T) of coal in 1860, but that had risen to a staggering 270 million t (245 million T) by 1900.

AMERICA'S WORKING CLASS

Titans of industry, such as Rockefeller, Carnegie, and others, left their mark on the U.S. economy during the last decades of the nineteenth and early twentieth centuries. In doing so, they became some of the wealthiest men in the country. But, for the vast majority of the working class in America, such wealth was unfathomable.

At the turn of the century the richest 1 percent of American families held seven out of every eight dollars of the U.S. economy, but 80 percent of families lived on the edge of poverty. For every family with an annual income greater than $50,000, 44 families lived on less than $500.

Many of the people who labored in the factories, mills, mines, and on the railroads owned by the great industrial giants did so in facilities where working conditions were appalling, while earning little for their labor. Between 1860 and 1890 the prices of many consumer goods declined and there were declines in the cost of living, while real wages and earnings in manufacturing went up around 50 percent during those same years. Real wages saw another 37 percent growth between 1890 and 1914. However, by 1900 the hourly wage in manufacturing was only about 21 cents and working conditions largely did not improve overall. Those same workers, then, went home to poor neighborhoods where they often lived in rundown tenement buildings.

To alleviate some of the labor problems—long hours, low wages, poor factory conditions—workers began to try to organize into unions and other organizations.

Some of these efforts dated back to earlier in the nineteenth century, with such groups as the Knights of Labor, founded in 1869, which was the country's first important national labor organization. This union invited all workers to join, both skilled and unskilled. Members included blacks and whites, men and women, foreign workers and native-born Americans. The Knights grew rapidly, reaching a membership of 700,000 by 1886, but soon declined, only to be replaced by another group, the American Federation of Labor (AFL). Other important union movements included the United Mine Workers (UMW), which organized in 1890.

Against the backdrop of this budding labor movement, several important strikes were called, including the Great Railroad Strike of 1877, which brought rail traffic to a virtual halt in the East and Midwest. U.S. Army troops were sent in to break the strike, and union membership fell sharply in its aftermath, from 300,000 to 50,000 workers.

Then, in May 1886, a hard-fought union struggle at the McCormick Reaper Works in Chicago ended in the famous Haymarket Riot, during which someone tossed a bomb, killing seven policemen. Eight anarchist leaders were tried and sentenced to death for this crime. Some of them were well-known in Chicago as labor agitators, such as August Spies. Spies committed suicide before he could be executed.

During the early 1890s two significant strikes took place: the Homestead Strike (1892) and the Pullman Strike (1894). The Homestead clash unfolded at the Carnegie Steel Company in Homestead, Pennsylvania, where workers went off the job and later fought detectives hired by company officials to take over the mill and run it. When 10 strikers were killed, the governor called in 8,000 state troops to stop the violence.

Two years later the Pullman Strike took place at the Pullman Car factory outside Chicago after workers' wages were cut, due to a depression that had begun in 1893. When the strike became a nationwide rail stoppage, the U.S. government weighed in, taking the side of the employers, since the strike interrupted the delivery of the U.S. mail. Again, federal troops were sent in, and the strike ended.

Overall, through the latter decades of the nineteenth century, labor organizations continued to struggle. One success of unions was the passage of laws against child labor. The National Labor Union, the Knights of Labor, and the AFL all fought to limit child worker abuse, and states began banning child labor during the 1890s. Some states capped the number of hours a child could be employed in a week and set up a minimum wage for young workers.

The Bessemer steel manufacturing process used oxidation to remove impurities from the molten iron. This process took place in large egg-shaped containers, called Bessemer converters, shown here in use at Carnegie's Pittsburgh steel works in 1886.

Everything Carnegie touched seemed to turn either to steel or to money. By 1900 his steel company holdings were producing more steel than all the companies in Great Britain, netting him a personal $40 million that year alone.

But, while Carnegie was a businessman, he was also a philanthropist. In 1889 he published a book, *The Gospel of Wealth,* in which he used the relatively new theory of Darwinism, and its "survival of the fittest" beliefs. Carnegie argued that as society had evolved, the differences between those who had accumulated wealth (the new millionaires) and the laboring class of workers was the true measure of how advanced that society had become. He wrote, "Not evil, but good, has come to the race from the accumulation of wealth by those who have the ability and energy that produces it." While Carnegie himself did not always allow for unlimited competition in the steel industry, he stated that competition was an important social phenomenon, "best for the race, because it insures the survival of the fittest in every department."

Yet, for Carnegie, the point of his life's work was not the accumulation of wealth, but the distribution of that wealth. For him, "The man who dies rich dies disgraced." The wealthy man must see to his needs, yes, (Carnegie saw to his own needs with a $40-million-a-year retirement income and a castle in Scotland), and to those of his family and dependents, but he should then consider the rest of his money as a "trust" held to benefit the public good.

Carnegie spent his later years giving away much of his wealth, including $60 million to establish public libraries and another $60 million to support education projects. He gave to universities, hospitals, parks, and meeting and concert halls. His point was that such things were not handouts to the masses, but provided opportunities for society's members to better themselves.

Morgan: the Financial Wizard

While Andrew Carnegie's story was one of rags-to-riches, Wall Street tycoon John Pierpont Morgan was born in Connecticut in 1837 into a wealthy family. Morgan's father already represented East Coast money, being an international banker. Completing his schooling in 1854, Pierpont, as he liked to be called, joined a New York financial firm and, by 1861, opened his own bank—J.P. Morgan & Company. During the Civil War, Morgan received a contract from the War Department, through which he bought up defective rifles, had them retooled, then sold them back to the government at a high profit.

Through the 1870s and 1880s Morgan was a partner in several financial firms, and he and his partners underwrote new issues of railroad stocks and bonds. Sometimes he brokered important deals between competing railroad companies and their officials, occasionally onboard his private yacht, the *Corsaire III*, on the Hudson River. The boat measured as long as a football field and boasted a crew of 70. Morgan once said, notes historian Harold Evans, about the newly rich men of his time, those with whom he rubbed shoulders, "You can do business with anyone, but you can only sail a boat with a gentleman."

Like Rockefeller, Morgan was no fan of corporate or industrial competition. When he and a business associate, James J. Hill, fought in 1901 with another railroad owner, Edward H. Harriman, over who might control the Chicago, Burlington & Quincy Railroad (CB&Q)—the key line serving Chicago, St. Paul-Minneapolis, and Omaha—others on Wall Street went into a panic. (Between the three titans, Hill and Morgan held control over the Great Northern Railroad and the Northern Pacific, while Harriman ran the Southern Pacific and the Union Pacific.) Morgan's answer was to provide Harriman with a management share of the CB&Q,

while he placed the GN, NP, and the CB&Q into one large railroad trust, the Northern Securities Corporation. All was well in Morgan's mind with this arrangement. The deal limited competition and cleared the road for the efficient and profitable operation of these railroads.

Railroads did not dominate Morgan's financial deal making, however. By the 1890s through his J.P. Morgan & Company, Pierpont was busy structuring and financing new industries, such as General Electric (GE), which came into existence in 1892. Just a few years later, he raised the capital to form American Telephone & Telegraph (AT&T), as well as International Harvester, a company based on the old McCormick Harvester Works.

But his ultimate coup was the 1901 purchase of Carnegie's steel company, consolidating it with other steel producers to become a giant conglomerate, a trust that formed America's first billion-dollar corporation—United States Steel. When Carnegie and Morgan finally set a purchase price for Carnegie's steel empire, the price tag being $492 million, Morgan told the Scottish tycoon, notes historian Richard Tedlow: "Mr. Carnegie, I want to congratulate you on being the richest man in the world."

By 1912 J. Pierpont Morgan was the leading financier-banker in the United States, holding 12 directorships in 47 corporations. Notes historian Ron Chernow, so powerful was Morgan that, when he was quoted that year saying, "America is good enough for me," presidential candidate William Jennings Bryan quipped: "Whenever he doesn't like it, he can give it back to us." Morgan's trust making was certainly not unique, however, with the exception, perhaps, of the scope of some of the corporate structures he brought together. The U.S. business world, by 1904, was home to 318 industrial trusts, capitalized with over $7 billion, representing nearly 5,300 separate production plants.

3

Gilded Age
Politics

The latter decades of the nineteenth century represented, in many ways, a political wasteland in America. The era would be remembered as one of corruption in politics; of widespread graft and dishonest political leaders. In 1879 a young Woodrow Wilson, later to become president, but then merely a recent college graduate, observed the poor condition of politics in America, notes historian George Tindall: "No leaders, no principles; no principles, no parties." There were parties, of course; the same two that dominate U.S. politics today, the Democrats and the Republicans. Prior to 1896, however, they were sometimes lookalike parties, with few clear differences between them. Neither party boasted a conspicuous positive program or agenda; both opposed the government limiting the power of big business; and both fought against attempts to limit corruption, until the hue and cry of the public simply became overwhelming.

THE DEMOCRATIC PARTY

While both the major parties might support similar platforms during the 1870s and 80s, they drew support from different constituencies. The Democrats relied, following Reconstruction, on the "Solid South," where white Southerners dominated the politics of the region. The Democrats also had support from the urban political machines, those party bosses who ran the Northern city governments, using graft and corruption as their primary political tactics. Both these support groups of the Democrat Party cared less about national issues and more about local or regional matters, such as ending Reconstruction, whether blacks could vote, or the level of patronage through government-issued contracts. As for additional constituencies, the Democrats relied on immigrants, including Catholics and Jews, as well as skeptics and freethinkers.

Even if the two major political parties did not seem to take the major issues of the day seriously, it appears that many Americans believed in casting their ballots anyway. While modern presidential elections often draw about half the eligible voters, voter turnout during the 1880s and 1890s ran much higher—between 70 and 80 percent. How was it, then, that voters came out in droves to vote for candidates who continuously dodged the larger issues? It appears that both voters and candidates thought at the time that they were seeing to the great political causes of their day, including money issues, tariffs, civil service reform, labor problems, and immigration. The members of each new Congress ultimately did take stands and cast their ballots regarding these issues, apparently often enough to satisfy significant numbers of voters.

The Democrats relied on presidential candidates who came from New York, where party leaders were as conservative as Republicans. But those Democrats regularly lost. In 1868 Horatio Seymour, New York governor during the Civil War, lost to Ulysses S. Grant, hero of the Army of the Potomac. In 1872 Grant defeated his Democrat challenger, Horace Greeley, editor of the *New York Tribune*. Next time around another Democrat New York governor, Samuel Tilden, lost an extremely controversial election to Republican Rutherford B. Hayes of Ohio. In fact, between 1856 and 1912, only one Democrat presidential candidate, Grover Cleveland, was elected to the White House, winning two non-consecutive terms in 1884 and 1892. Cleveland was also from New York.

THE REPUBLICAN PARTY

By contrast, the Republican Party relied on support from mainline Protestant groups, especially those of British origin. Republicans also received votes from more reform-minded individuals, just as they had from abolitionists before the Civil War. They relied on support from Midwestern farmers, black voters from the South, and especially from Northern veterans of the Civil War, those who had fought on behalf of the Grand Army of the Republic. Republicans also had the general backing of factory owners and other manufacturers, due to their support of protective tariffs.

When Republican party leaders went out to speak on behalf of their party's candidates, whether for president or some minor state or local office, they constantly reminded voters that the Republicans had created the Homestead Act that provided free western land to American citizens and immigrants alike. They also made a practice of telling voters that the Democrats represented the party of secession and the Confederacy, since most Southerners belonged to that political party. This tactic was called "waving the bloody shirt," and it was used in elections for decades following the Civil War. Above all, the Republicans constantly connected themselves to their great martyred leader, President Abraham Lincoln. Lincoln became the great symbol of honest leadership and sacrificial service to his country, and Republicans were more than eager to capitalize on his legacy.

But, Lincoln's legacy aside, the Republican Party of the 1870s was a fragmented organization representing at least three groups, some less honorable and upright than others. The honest wing of the party was called the "Mugwumps," as their critics often accused them of failing to take strong stands on the issues, claiming they "sat on the fence," with their "mug" on one side, and their "wump" on the other. Nevertheless, the Mugwumps fought hard against party corruption. The most corrupt wing was the seemingly misnamed group called the "Stalwarts," representing politicians who sought party influence and government patronage for their supporters. The Stalwarts were led by New York Senator Roscoe Conkling. He was a flamboyant figure, but he was ruthless. He summed politics up as "a rotten business" in which "nothing counts except to win."

The third wing of the Republicans was known as the "Half-Breeds," led by Senator James G. Blaine from Maine. The Half-Breeds were corrupt and wanted to peddle influence, just as the Stalwarts did, but they often tried to cover up their actions, hoping to present the appearance of honesty. Often, the Stalwarts and Half-Breeds allied together, if for no other reason than to push along the careers of Blaine and Conkling.

Patronage

Much of the innate corruption of both the Republicans and the Democrats was centered on the practice of patronage. During these latter decades of the nineteenth century political patronage was commonplace. Members of both parties secured federal jobs for those who helped get them elected.

In 1881, for example, approximately half of the federal, non-elected offices—around 56,000 positions—were awarded as patronage. Following his election as president in 1884, Democrat Grover Cleveland replaced nearly 40,000 postmasters across the country with those Democrats who were loyal to the party. And Cleveland was a president often quoted for stating: "A public office is a public trust."

A CYCLE OF ELECTIONS

In 1876, following Republican Rutherford B. Hayes's defeat of New York Democrat Samuel Tilden, the new president took office with a variety of goals in mind. Through the controversial election, with its disputed dual sets of ballots from four contested states, Hayes had won the White House only with a promise made to the Democrats that the Republicans would immediately end Reconstruction. Hayes wasted no time in doing just that. But he still faced four difficult years in the White House. During his presidency, the Democrats controlled the House and, after the off-year election in 1878, the Senate was also in Democratic hands, helping to block moves made by the Republican leader.

Hayes, though, made some important decisions as president. After appointing a former Confederate to his cabinet and withdrawing the last federal troops from the South, he began to take serious steps toward reforming the civil service. He did not like the system of patronage, which encouraged individuals to show up almost daily at the White House looking for a political appointment, everything from county official to ambassador. To show his true colors, Hayes refused to follow the common, longstanding practice of discharging thousands of officeholders and replacing them with his political favorites. In fact, one of his cabinet members, Carl Schurz, introduced a merit system for filling positions in the Department of the Interior, an infant step toward civil service reform. Otherwise, Hayes was a conservative politician, one who vetoed the Bland–Allison Act, which was designed to increase the nation's money supply. Earlier in his presidency, he sent in troops to put down the Great Railroad Strike of 1877. The troops seriously injured or killed more than 25 strikers in Baltimore and Chicago.

Elected, but Never President

In 1880 Hayes chose not to run for a second term, and the Stalwarts and Half-Breeds were left with the nomination up for grabs. Conkling and the Stalwarts pushed for Grant to be renominated, but the Half-Breeds supported Blaine, deadlocking the Republican convention. Then, Wisconsin changed its votes in support of the Speaker of the House, James A. Garfield. The Stalwarts got their man for vice president though—the notoriously corrupt New York Customs Superintendent, Chester A. Arthur.

Garfield was a reluctant candidate, but accepted the nomination. He was an honest man, a classics professor and part-time lay minister in a fundamentalist religious group, known as the Disciples of Christ. [The group is less fundamentalist today.] He was also a Civil War veteran. The Democrats were not to be outdone. They, too, selected a veteran officer of the war, a Pennsylvanian named Winfield Scott Hancock, whose men had faced off against Pickett's forces during the battle of Gettysburg. The party ran Garfield as a common man, born in a log cabin, and who had worked as a canal boat horse driver, known as a hoggie. The candidate's slogan had been "From the Towpath to the White House."

Throughout the campaign neither candidate talked about the issues, which included such national concerns as labor legislation, the regulation of railroads, an income tax, and money issues. Garfield won, but barely. Although nearly 9 million votes were cast, the two candidates were separated

This contemporary engraving depicts the Garfield Assassination on July 2, 1881. Guiteau is shown shooting President Garfield, who had then been in office for just four months. The figure at right is the secretary of state, James G. Blaine.

by fewer than 39,000 votes. A third party, the Greenback-Labor Party, had run their own candidate, James B. Weaver, but received very few votes.

Unfortunately, Garfield never had his opportunity as president. He was shot by a mentally unbalanced man, named Charles Guiteau, in the Baltimore and Potomac Railroad Station outside Washington in 1881. Garfield struggled to remain alive for two months, but finally succumbed to blood poisoning.

A Reformed Character

Suddenly, the formerly corrupt New York official, Vice President Chester Arthur, was president. Arthur was an intelligent man, a Phi Beta Kappa graduate of Union College, also known for his flamboyant wardrobe in the style of Roscoe Conkling, his patron. The Stalwarts believed they had gained the presidency as their own. But Arthur immediately disappointed the corrupt Republican wingmen. He said, as noted by historian Tindall: "For the vice-presidency I was indebted to Mr. Conkling, but for the presidency of the United States my debt is to the Almighty."

Few American political leaders have ever made such dramatic changes as President Arthur. He soon became known as a civil service supporter and a tariff reformer. Through the next year he gave his support, much to the chagrin of the Stalwarts, to a reform bill proposed by a Democrat senator from Ohio, "Gentleman George" Pendleton. Passed in January 1883, the Pendleton Civil Service Act set up a three-man Civil Service Commission—a completely new type of federal agency. Under the commission's direction, approximately one-eighth of government, non-elected jobs were to be filled through competitive examinations by candidates. The act also allowed the president to add to the number of jobs under the act at his discretion.

The presidency had been a time of redemption for Arthur, but it cost him the support of Roscoe Conkling and the Stalwarts. In 1884 the Republicans dumped Arthur and offered the nomination to Senator James G. Blaine, whose day as the leader of the Half-Breeds had arrived. Blaine was a colorful politician, who gave memorable speeches and was known for using his political power for personal profit. When Blaine approached Conkling to campaign for him, the Stalwart leader only sneered, notes historian Richard Hofstadter: "No thank you, I don't engage in criminal practice." With Blaine's nomination, the Mugwumps bolted from the party and even supported the Democratic challenger, a New Yorker and former governor, named Stephen Grover Cleveland. Known as an honest, courageous, independent-minded, yet stubborn politician, Cleveland was a man of principle.

A Democratic President

The election proved a close one, with Cleveland taking 219 electoral votes to Blaine's 182. The difference in the popular vote for each candidate was only about 23,000 votes. Cleveland proved to be an effective president. Famous for saying "a public office is public trust," he supported civil service reform, taking the opportunity under the Pendleton Act to double the number of federal jobs on the list covered by the act. Ahead of his time when it came to conservation, Cleveland recovered large tracts of mostly western public land that was being illegally held by railroads, lumber companies, cattle ranchers, and mining consortiums. In 1887 he sent a bill to Congress that ultimately created the federal Division of the Forestry.

Cleveland also took on various special interest groups during his presidency. Back in 1862 Congress had passed the first Civil War pension law to provide for those soldiers disabled during their wartime service, as well as their orphans and widows. Twenty years later, however, Congressmen were now okaying pension bills for any disability a veteran of the Grand Army of the Republic might have. In 1887 Cleveland vetoed a new Dependent Pension bill that would have handed out monies to an endless number of veterans and their family members, as well as many cheats and frauds.

President Cleveland also tried to rein in another special interest group by advocating railroad regulation. The power of the nation's railroads and their various presidents and boards had grown phenomenally over the years, and Cleveland was ready to put the brakes on some of the unbridled power they represented.

To that end, he supported an act creating the Interstate Commerce Commission (ICC), the first significant, federal regulatory agency in U.S. history. The new law was brought about by pressure from small business people and farmers across the country who felt they were being victimized by the railroads. It made it illegal for railroads to make pooling arrangements, in which several railroad heads agreed to charge the same freight rates, thus ending real competition. The law intended to end railroad rebates to big customers and the charging of higher rates for a short haul (per ton per mile) compared to a long haul. The railroads were also supposed to publicly post their freight rates. While the ICC did not have much power to force railroads to behave differently, the new law was the start of federal regulation of railroads and a host of other public entities over the years to come.

Grandson of a President

In 1888 satisfied Democrats renominated the "reformer" Grover Cleveland. The Republicans, on the other hand, selected an almost unknown Indiana lawyer named Benjamin Harrison, whose claim to fame was that his grandfather, William Henry Harrison, had been president. Harrison was also a Civil War veteran and had accomplished so little politically since his election to the Senate in 1880, that his record could not offend anyone.

The campaign proved one of the most corrupt in U.S. history, even if the candidates themselves were not. The Republicans leaned on big business for support, taking in a campaign war chest of $4 million—an immense sum at that time. They also promised veterans more general pension bills. But both parties also campaigned on the protective tariff issue, with Harrison supporting high tariffs and Cleveland having already supported the lowering of tariff duties during his presidency. Ultimately the election results proved awkward. Cleveland gained 100,000 more popular votes than Harrison, but the Republican candidate captured key states (one of them was Harrison's home state of Indiana), giving him the electoral college majority he needed (233–168) to win the election.

Harrison, as president, enjoyed Republican majorities in both houses of Congress during his first two years in office. He fought for further civil service reform, adding another 11,000 offices to the list of classified government jobs that were to be filled through civil service exams. Congress remained busy during those two years, with six western territories gaining statehood—North and South Dakota, Montana, Wyoming, Idaho, and Washington. The territory of Oklahoma was also established under the Organic Act.

Congress also passed an important piece of legislation with Harrison's support. The Sherman Antitrust Act made monopolistic business practices illegal. In addition, Congress enacted the McKinley Tariff Act, designed to protect U.S. businesses and manufacturers. But the new law caused higher prices in the United States and contributed to the depression of 1893. Also, legislators passed the Dependent Pension Act (1890) which gave a pension to all veterans of the

Grand Army of the Republic suffering from any disability, no matter if it was the result of war service or not, and to all their widows. The program was a huge handout that increased the number of pensioners to almost 1 million, at an annual cost of nearly $160 million. Congress also passed the Sherman Silver Purchase Act (1890), which had been pushed by western silver interests. The act increased the amount of silver purchased by the federal treasury to 4.5 million ounces (128 million grams) monthly.

In foreign policy, the Harrison administration pursued increased trade with foreign nations, which was greatly supported by the nation's manufacturing interests. The United States called for the first conference of nations in the Western Hemisphere, the Pan American Conference, in 1889, where U.S. officials courted trade agreements with their Latin American neighbors. Harrison also facilitated the annexation of Hawaii as a U.S. territory during his term, following the overthrow of the Hawaiian queen through a revolution that was backed and financed by U.S. planters and businessmen on the islands. The President's representatives did negotiate a treaty with Hawaii, but Harrison left office before it was ratified by the Senate. In 1892 Harrison ran for a second term, but was defeated by Grover Cleveland, his old opponent from 1888. (Cleveland thus became the only president to serve two non-consecutive terms.)

THE PLIGHT OF THE FARMERS

Throughout the latter decades of the nineteenth century, life changed dramatically for the vast majority of Americans. One group that experienced significant differences to their way of life was the country's farmers. New machinery and farming techniques now made farmers more productive than they had been before. Through technology—including the introduction of such machines as mechanical reapers and binders, steam-powered threshing machines, and a host of other farm-related inventions—a single U.S. farmer could be between 10 and 20 times more productive by the 1890s than he had been during the 1860s.

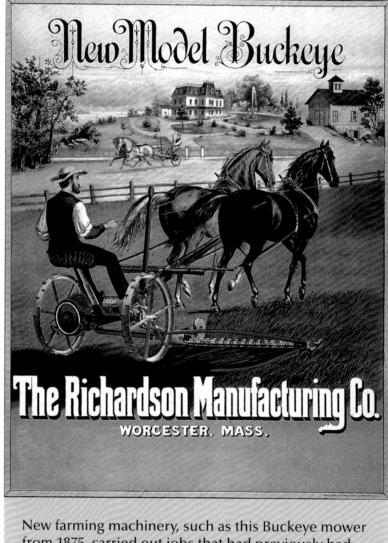

New farming machinery, such as this Buckeye mower from 1875, carried out jobs that had previously had to be done by hand. Some Buckeye models could cut wheat, pack it in a bundle, and wrap it in twine.

However, following the Civil War, farmers had struggled with a variety of difficult circumstances, including mistreatment at the hands of the nation's railroads, high prices for everything they needed on the farm, and low commodity prices. These circumstances led farmers to organize as they had never done before. During the late 1860s Oliver Hudson Kelley founded the Patrons of Husbandry, commonly referred to as "The Grange." This organization sought to answer some of the farmers' overarching problems. By the mid-1870s some 1.5 million farmers, mostly in the Midwest, had joined the Grange.

SILVER AND GOLD

One constant problem for farmers during the period from the 1870s until the 1890s was that of money. Farmers generally believed that farm commodity prices were dropping through those decades because of a shortage in the nation's money supply. (In reality, prices fell because farmers, aided by new technologies and farming methods, overproduced.) But the call for more money in circulation led many farmers to support keeping greenbacks. Greenbacks were paper bills, produced during the Civil War as a means of paying for war purchases by the government. But they were not redeemable in specie (gold or silver) and their value was based only on the good faith of the federal government.

The government agreed to "buy back" all greenbacks in gold. But many people did not bother, since their paper money could be redeemed at any time for specie. As a result, the government allowed more than a third of a billion dollars in greenbacks to remain in circulation. For farmers this was not enough.

Many such "cheap money" advocates began to clamor for the government to mint greater numbers of silver coins, just as it did gold coins. At that time, coins made of silver or gold were worth their face value, because the metal in the coin was equal in value to that amount. In other words, a $20 gold piece was worth that amount because it contained $20 worth of gold. However, with so much silver being mined in the West during the 1870s and 1880s, the true value of silver was dropping at an alarming rate, making silver a shaky metal on which to base a part of the nation's money supply. Still, farmers and others continued their chant.

The government responded—sort of. In 1878 Congress passed the Bland–Allison Act, which authorized the U.S. Treasury Department to buy and mint between $2 and $4 million worth of silver each month. The act ultimately provided a market for silver producers in the West, but the government, after purchasing the silver, did not mint much of it into coins.

In the meantime, farm prices continued to tumble. Wheat that had sold for $2.50 a bushel in 1868 dropped to just 78 cents by the late 1880s. Corn fell to 15 cents a bushel, and cotton plummeted from 65 cents a pound to only 5 cents by 1895. Farmers were desperate, facing high interest rates on their mortgages and low commodity prices. A 10-year drought cycle across the Great Plains, starting in 1886, only added insult to injury.

Congress seemed to respond to the money issues in 1890, when it replaced the Bland–Allison Act with a new piece of legislation—the Sherman Silver Purchase Act. This act required the Treasury to buy 4.5 million ounces (128 million grams) of silver monthly at the market price, and to pay for these silver purchases with paper money that was redeemable in gold or silver. For the moment, cheap money supporters, the group often referred to as the "Silverites," were in tall cotton. But the act changed little. Most of the silver purchased by the government was not coined, and the money supply remained static.

A PARTY OF POPULISTS

Fed up, farmers and others formed a third political party the following year. It came out of a meeting of Farmer's Alliance leaders, most of whom came from the Midwest and Far West. They launched the People's Party, or the

COLORFUL POPULISTS

Throughout the 1892 election campaign, huge crowds of farmers gathered across the Great Plains and the South at outdoor rallies, picnics, barbecues, and fish fries to hear Populist speakers, including James B. Weaver, whose words were often eloquent and stirring.

Populist leaders included such colorful individuals as Mary Elizabeth Lease from Kansas, who strongly suggested to farmers, notes historian O. Gene Clanton, "to raise less corn and more hell." Raised by Irish immigrant farmers, Lease had become a lawyer, studying law while, notes Clanton, "pinning sheets of notes above her wash tub." Her voice was so loud and forceful that her critics referred to her as "Mary Yellin."

Another colorful Kansas Populist was Jeremiah "Sockless Jerry" Simpson. Originally from Canada, Simpson moved to Kansas, where he struggled in the farming and cattle business. In 1890 he ran for Congress, with Mary Lease's campaign support.

Simpson cut an interesting figure, a highly intelligent man with pale blue eyes and large calloused hands. His nickname, "Sockless Jerry," came about during the election, when he accused his Republican opponent of wearing silk stockings. His rival retaliated by accusing Simpson of not wearing any socks at all. With Mary Lease's encouragement, the new nickname stuck.

Simpson was popular for both his rhetoric and his pro-farm politics. He once said to Republicans who tried to shrug off the new farmer party, notes historian Richard F. Snow: "You can't put this movement down by sneers or by ridicule, for its foundation was laid as far back as the foundation of the world. It is a struggle between the robbers and the robbed."

Populist Party, in Cincinnati, Ohio. In 1892, an election year, the Populists met in Omaha, Nebraska, and prepared to run their own candidate for president. On July 4 they adopted the party's platform that included far-reaching goals and reforms: 1) an increase in the money supply, 2) government ownership of the nation's railroads, telegraphs, and telephones, 3) the return of surplus government land by railroads and other businesses, 4) a graduated income tax, 5) a system of government-owned warehouses and grain elevators to be used by farmers, and 6) various political reforms including the direct election of U.S. senators and the adoption of the secret ballot, the initiative, and the referendum. These policies helped the Populists to gain support not only from farmers, but from factory workers and other wage earners. The platform also demanded shorter working hours and restrictions on immigration. Critics of the Populist platform referred to the party's members as "Hayseed Socialists."

ECONOMIC COLLAPSE

Although President Cleveland began his second term with great support across the country, he soon found himself presiding over a nation in a deep financial depression, beginning in 1893. The depression lasted through his entire term. When the country faced a serious gold drain, due to a pull-out of European investors in the U.S. economy, Cleveland struck a deal with Wall Street financiers to provide gold for the nation's dwindling reserves. The move probably saved the nation's economy, which made a gradual recovery. While financial issues dominated the Cleveland administration at home, the United States began to pursue foreign policy goals. Cleveland inherited the bill before Congress to annex the Hawaiian Islands, but he did not support the annexation and did not pursue the passage of the treaty. His administration also became involved in a boundary dispute in South America between Venezuela and Great Britain. When Cleveland seemed to threaten U.S. military involvement in the affair, Great Britain agreed to allow an arbitration board to decide the issue at hand. The crisis soon passed. In 1896 Cleveland, having served two terms, chose not to seek another.

A NEW WAY OF CAMPAIGNING

With the field wide open, both the Democrats and Republicans scrambled for candidates in 1896. The Republicans landed on the governor of Ohio, William McKinley, whom some had supported for the party's nomination back in 1892. He had served in the House of Representatives between 1876 and 1891, where his support of high tariffs led to one being named after him. He had also supported the expanded circulation of silver coinage over gold, yet the party platform in 1896 included a call for the nation to establish a gold standard and drop silver coins from circulation.

The Democrats chose William J. Bryan, a strong Baptist from Nebraska who supported an expansion of the nation's money supply through the free coinage of silver. Prior to 1896, he had served two terms in the House of Representatives. In selecting the Midwestern, silverite Bryan, the Democrats stole much of the Populist Party's thunder. When the Populists met at convention in St. Louis two weeks after the Democratic convention, they, too, chose Bryan as their candidate, since selecting someone else would only have split the silver vote.

At the Democratic convention, Bryan had won over many of the delegates with a speech he delivered against the gold standard. In his address, he reminded those present that America owed great debts to its farmers and simple laborers. He extolled the virtues of the Midwest and its agrarian roots, while scolding the "financial magnates" back East. Using highly religious metaphors, Bryan's "Cross of Gold" speech concluded with the lines: "You shall not press down upon the brow of labor this crown of thorns. You shall not crucify mankind upon a cross of gold!" As Bryan ended his speech, the majority of the 20,000 delegates gathered jumped to their feet in applause and adulation, many with tears streaming down their cheeks.

The two candidates, representing three parties, pursued extremely different campaigns. McKinley's was more traditional, amounting to his staying home and engaging in a "front porch" campaign. In the meantime, Bryan crisscrossed the country by train, delivering 600 speeches before 5 million people in 27 states. Bryan's battle proved to run only uphill. Nearly every important U.S. newspaper supported the Republicans. At many factories, workers paid on the Saturday before the election received a warning with their pay, similar to that written by the owner of the Steinway Piano Works, notes historian Paul Boller: "Men, vote as you please, but if Bryan is elected... the whistle will not blow Wednesday morning."

Despite Bryan's crusading across the country in favor of an increase in silver in the nation's money supply, McKinley managed to defeat him by more than a half million votes (7.1 million to 6.5 million), with an electoral vote of 271 to 176. Bryan had carried most of the West and the South, but had not gained much support north of the Ohio and Potomac Rivers. In the big cities, he had run poorly. Bryan's defeat was also a defeat for the Populists, and their power soon ended. But the call for reform would find its voice in a new political party, one that would take root during the early 1900s, demanding many of the same reforms the Populists had—the Progressive Party.

4

The Spanish-American War

Throughout nearly all the nineteenth century the vast majority of Americans remained content to look inward. Each passing generation took a view that the United States was a developing nation; one with great expanses of land just waiting for U.S. expansionism. Most were content to build the nation's great cities, lay claim to the West, lay the foundations for mile markers of progress—roads, canals, railroads, factories, and watermills—across the U.S. landscape. Most had little interest in the problems of other nations, including their wars, international political intrigues, or colonizing efforts. Since the days of George Washington, who warned Americans in the 1790s against becoming entangled in European alliances, the United States had, with a handful of notable exceptions, steered clear of foreign political ties. Yes, the United States had bought Alaska from the Russians during the 1860s, and established a naval base on the Pacific Island of Samoa by treaty during the late 1870s, and wrote up trade agreements with Hawaii, but these represented small blips on the radar of American foreign policy.

A CHANGE OF ATTITUDE

However, the latter years of the nineteenth century delivered a change of attitude among significant numbers of Americans, who suddenly recognized the need to promote U.S. interests overseas. Two factors played into this alternative view. Americans had developed a complex economic and production system, including factories and transportation systems, much of it mechanized, which produced such large numbers of consumer goods that new markets were needed overseas. This expanded industrial base also had a hunger for the natural resources of other countries—rubber, tin, sugar, wood, and hundreds of other materials—needed to create finished goods in America. Secondly, some Americans were looking jealously at the various European powers that were scrambling for colonies in Asia, Africa, and sometimes even Latin America. The colonizing powers could create new markets, build new coaling stations for their ships, and control new sources of raw materials.

Americans had rarely taken seriously the idea of establishing colonies overseas. Even when Hawaii fell into America's lap during the early 1890s, President Cleveland did not support its annexation as a territory. But some Americans were beginning to view the need for overseas colonies with a more discerning eye. For those who saw the need for such foreign advancement on the part of the United States, a book published in 1890 had a significant impact. Alfred T. Mahan's study titled *The Influence of Sea Power Upon World History, 1660–1783*, suggested that no country could ever maintain commercial expansion overseas without the backing of a powerful navy. In 1890 America did not have one.

Such readers of Mahan's book as McKinley's assistant secretary of the navy, Theodore Roosevelt, and McKinley's secretary of state, John Hay, became strong believers in the need to build up the American navy while encouraging U.S. expansionism overseas. With Roosevelt's fingerprints all over it, the U.S. Navy had either built or authorized the construction of 11 new battleships by 1896.

This cartoon from 1897, entitled *Patient Waiters Are No Losers*, illustrates U.S. foreign policy of the period. A patient Uncle Sam is shown waiting for new territories, including Cuba, Canada, and Hawaii, to fall into his possession.

For others the 1890s seemed right for such action over-seas. Christian groups thought the peoples of Africa and Asia needed to be taught Christianity, so they sent out missionaries to these foreign and "heathen" places. Many white Anglo-Saxons of all creeds had similar objectives—they felt that western culture should be taken to the primitive parts of the world to improve the lives of the natives living there. Americans no longer looked at other countries as places to avoid, but saw them as markets, new locations to plant the flag of democracy, while saving their souls to boot.

"CUBA LIBRE"

Perhaps no place in the world drew the attention of more Americans by the mid-1890s than the island nation of Cuba, located just 70 miles (113 km) south of Florida's Key West. For 400 years, since the days of Columbus, Spain had held Cuba as a colony, tapping her natural resources, some-times enslaving her people, and taking the profits for itself. Cubans had come to resent Spanish rule as repressive and corrupt. During the 1860s a revolution had broken out, one that Spanish officials crushed immediately. But, a genera-tion later, circumstances seemed right for a return to Cuban revolution. By the early 1890s, as America struggled through a severe depression, U.S. businessmen reduced their trade in Cuban sugar, hurting the islands' inhabitants. By 1895 a new Cuban revolutionary movement was afoot, called *Cuba Libre,* "Free Cuba." This time Americans took notice.

As Spain struck back at the revolutionaries on the island, people in the United States became increasingly sympa-thetic to the plight of the Cuban people. Many Americans held animosities toward the Spanish. They were particular-ly touched by stories that filtered out of the island about Spanish atrocities. One name in particular became synony-mous with villainy to Americans. A Spanish general by the name of Valeriano Weyler became notorious for rounding up 300,000 Cubans, many from remote jungle villages, and placing them in concentration camps, known as *reconcentrado*. There, large numbers of people died, many from disease, some from starvation. His reputation became so black that the Spanish general was known in U.S. newspapers as "the Butcher Weyler."

Another factor that drew Americans' attention toward the Cuban Revolution was the level of U.S. investment in Cuba. Primarily centered in the island's lucrative sugar market, U.S. businessmen had invested at least $50 million in Cuba, perhaps more. In 1890 the McKinley Tariff Act had allowed Cuban sugar to enter the United States duty free. So what happened next in Cuba was of great interest to an increasing number of Americans.

U.S. newspaper publishers did their part in lathering up American interest in Cuba's struggle for freedom. During the 1890s most Americans received one of the country's 14,000 weekly or 2,000 daily papers. From San Francisco to Helena, and Grand Rapids to New York, newspapers splashed stories across their pages of Spanish crimes against innocent Cubans. Sometimes such big-time newspaper owners and publishers as William Randolph Hearst or Joseph Pulitzer wanted simply to inflame U.S. opinion in favor of the Cubans and against the Spanish. Lurid stories out of Cuba sold lots of newspapers. In New York City, Hearst's *New York Journal* and Pulitzer's *New York World* fought a war of the newsboys as they reported the latest from the Cuban front.

MCKINLEY AND WAR FEVER

William McKinley prepared to take the office of the president in March 1897 against the backdrop of war fever in America. He had campaigned in favor of Cuban independence, annexation of Hawaii, and even the building of a canal across the

Isthmus of Panama. Yet he was opposed to taking the United States into any direct conflict with the Spanish, even in support of Cuban independence. After all, the United States was just emerging from the deep economic depression that had gripped the nation since 1893. But, by 1898, several events drew McKinley and the American people toward war.

On February 9, U.S. newspapers published a private letter written by the Spanish minister to the United States, Dupuy DeLome. Writing to a friend, DeLome had referred to President McKinley, notes historian George Tindall, as "weak and a bidder for the admiration of the crowd." He called the

WHAT HAPPENED TO THE *MAINE*?

No event served as a greater catalyst for the United States entering into a war with Spain than the mysterious destruction of the USS *Maine*. Despite repeated efforts to determine the exact cause of the explosion onboard the great U.S. battleship, doubts about what happened still remain.

Immediately following the sinking of the *Maine,* the Spanish held an official inquiry to find the cause. Their findings determined that the cause of the explosion was internal, and not caused by a mine detonated on the ship's exterior. But a subsequent U.S. naval investigation disagreed, giving the cause as an external explosion, perhaps similar to one caused by a

mine, and even determined the point on the ship's hull where the damage had taken place.

Over the following 12 years the ship's wreckage remained in Havana Harbor, slowly sinking into the mud until only a small amount of twisted metal and the ship's aft mast were visible above the waterline.

Then, in 1910, a group of Americans petitioned the U.S. government for the *Maine* to be removed, and for the bodies of scores of American sailors who had never received a proper burial to be retrieved. During the removal of the hulk, the Army Corps of Engineers carried out another investigation and, president a "would-be politician." These hardly should have seemed like fighting words, as McKinley's own assistant secretary of the navy, Theodore Roosevelt, had already spoken out about the president, calling him "white-livered," having "no more backbone than a chocolate éclair." But Roosevelt's comments had been kept private. The Spanish minister's words—even though they were written in a letter that had been stolen and was not intended for the public—had not. The "DeLome Letter" only fueled the fire for war.

With tensions high across the United States, less than a week later the event occurred that was to prove critical in

by November 1911, determined that an external explosion had destroyed the ill-fated battleship. However the 1911 report did not agree with the 1898 report regarding the specific location where the explosion had been centered. In the meantime human remains were removed from the wreckage and later buried back in the United States.

By the spring of 1912 the remains of the *Maine* had been repaired adequately for the ship to be refloated. She was towed out to sea to a distance of 4 miles (6 km) from Cuba and sunk in about 1,800 ft (550 m) of water.

But the story of the *Maine* and her initial fate did not disappear forever. In 1976 a retired U.S. Navy admiral,

Hyman G. Rickover, took up a personal investigation of the *Maine's* destruction. Using explosives experts and the photographs of the wreck taken in 1911, he determined the ship had been destroyed, not by an external mine, but by a spontaneous combustion of coal dust in the ship's coal bunker, which was located next to the ship's powder magazine.

So, what did happen to the *Maine?* No one really knows. Critics of Rickover's report doubt his claim, stating that experts in both 1898 and 1911 would not have overlooked evidence of a coal dust explosion. Thus, the final mystery of the *Maine*, why the battleship exploded and who was responsible, will likely remain just that—a mystery.

leading America to arms against Spain. On February 15 the U.S. battleship *Maine* suddenly exploded in Havana Harbor, with the loss of more than 250 American servicemen. While no one could have known at the time exactly why the *Maine* had exploded, U.S. newspapers pretended they knew the cause—a Spanish underwater mine. Suddenly Americans were crying "Remember the *Maine*, To Hell with Spain!"

SPANISH CONCESSIONS, AMERICAN DECLARATIONS

Within days of the destruction of the *Maine*, Hearst's New York Journal reported with excitement: "The whole country thrills with war fever." Roosevelt blamed the Spanish unquestioningly. As for McKinley, he was not thrilled at all. He told one of his aides, notes historian George Tindall: "I have been through one war. I have seen the dead piled up, and I do not want to see another." But public pressure was impossible for the president to ignore. In March a naval court of inquiry determined that the *Maine* had sunk due to an external mine that had ignited the ship's powder magazine, although the court did not lay blame on Spain, or anyone else. In late March, with McKinley's approval, U.S. State Department officials delivered an ultimatum to the Spanish government that included the following demands: 1) that all fighting cease between Spain and the Cubans and that Spain grant an armistice to the revolutionaries, 2) Spain must then sit down with the Cubans to negotiate either self-government or independence, and 3) the concentration camps must be closed down.

Feeling the pressure from the U.S. government and knowing that the American people were calling for war, the Spanish government accepted the terms of the ultimatum on April 9. They only hedged on the question of complete Cuban independence. Yet, despite Spain's cooperation, on April 11,

1898, President McKinley stepped before a joint session of Congress to ask for a declaration of war against Spain. War spirit had finally engulfed even the reluctant President of the United States. Congressmen debated going to war for two weeks and finally adopted a formal declaration on April 25. To make clear to the people of the United States and the world that the country was going to war strictly to liberate Cuba, Congress adopted the Teller Amendment, which guaranteed Cuban independence.

INVADING THE PHILIPPINES

As the United States entered a war against Spain in support of independence for Cuba, the fighting opened, oddly enough, in the Pacific. Assistant Secretary of the Navy Theodore Roosevelt sent a cable message to Commodore George Dewey, whose Pacific fleet was anchored in Hong Kong, instructing Dewey to take action. The U.S. naval commander immediately steamed his fleet of six ships toward the Philippines, a large Pacific Island chain colonized by the Spanish for nearly as long as Cuba had been. On the night of April 30, under cover of darkness, Dewey sailed his ships past the aging Spanish fortress at Corregidor that guarded the entrance to Manila Bay. At dawn the following morning, U.S. gunners opened a barrage of fire, resulting in a Spanish defeat, including the loss of 170 men and their entire fleet of rusty, out-of-date ships. Only one American died, of heatstroke, in the boiler room of one of the U.S. ships.

Once ashore, Commodore Dewey met with and armed a band of Filipinos led by Emilio Aguinaldo, forming an alliance between the two opponents to Spanish colonial power. Americans explained that they had entered the war to help the Cubans gain their independence and that they had no territorial ambitions otherwise. Fighting continued through the next two months until U.S. transport ships loaded with troops reached the Philippines. On August 13 Spanish officials in Manila surrendered.

FIGHTING ON CUBAN SOIL

As action was taking place in the Pacific, additional dramas of war were unfolding in the Caribbean. The Spanish Atlantic Fleet, under the command of Admiral Pascual Cervera, had sailed out of the Cape Verde Islands. The Spanish had reached Santiago, Cuba, where the ships refueled. Then U.S. naval vessels, commanded by Admiral William T. Sampson, caught up with them. For the moment, the Spanish fleet remained in the relative shelter of Santiago Harbor.

The naval battle at Manila Bay, on May 1, 1898, was the first major engagement of the Spanish–American War. The ship shown in the left foreground is the USS *Olympia*, Commodore Dewey's flagship.

Most of the fighting during the summer of 1898 would involve many more U.S. soldiers than sailors, however. When the war opened the U.S. military was woefully unprepared, with only 28,000 men in uniform, many of whom were stationed across the West in various forts. McKinley issued a call for 125,000 volunteers to help in the coming fight, only to have 1 million men do so! The vast majority of them never saw the war, however, since the conflict was over by the end of that same summer. In the meantime, in early June, President McKinley dispatched the Fifth Army Corps, commanded by Major General William R. Shafter, to Santiago, Cuba.

Roosevelt Goes to War

One would-be soldier who did see action in Cuba was Theodore Roosevelt. With the outbreak of hostilities he had immediately resigned his post and formed a volunteer cavalry unit. They were officially called the "Rocky Mountain Riders," but everyone knew them as the "Rough Riders." Roosevelt called on old friends, including Harvard pals with whom he had played polo or football, Dakota cowboys, rangers, buffalo hunters, hard-edged ex-convicts, and western Indians, creating a colorful group of troops, indeed. Even the Rough Riders' chaplain believed a man who cheated at cards should be shot. The former navy assistant secretary had clamored for war for many months prior to the spring of 1898 and was ready, he said, notes historian George Tindall, to get "in on the fun" and "to act up to my preachings."

To prepare himself for Caribbean combat, Roosevelt visited the prestigious New York tailoring firm Brooks Brothers and ordered a custom-made, khaki-colored uniform. Since he was dreadfully nearsighted, he took along a dozen pairs of glasses as he departed with his cavalry buddies from Tampa, Florida, bound for Cuba.

When Roosevelt and his men landed in Cuba, Roosevelt wrote: "We disembarked with our rifles, our ammunition belts, and not much else. I carried some food in my pocket, and a light coat which was my sole camp equipment for the next three days." Although Roosevelt had managed to cut through enough red tape to get his men delivered to Cuba for the coming fight, they suffered supply problems just like everyone else.

San Juan and Kettle Hill

Ultimately the U.S. Army delivered close to 17,000 troops to Cuba. On the island the Spanish army numbered over 125,000 men. Many U.S. forces were ill-equipped, issued with heavy, woolen uniforms. While regular army troops were issued the latest .30 caliber Krag-Jørgenson rifles, national guard and volunteer forces carried, in many cases, Civil War-era Springfield rifles that still used black powder. Such guns, when fired, emitted a thick cloud of whitish smoke, which helped Spanish troops spot their enemies during fighting in the jungles of Cuba. The Spanish carried rifles that used smokeless cartridges.

When enough U.S. soldiers had arrived in Cuba, their objective became the capture of Santiago, where the Spanish fleet was docked. On June 20 Shafter marched his forces west of their coastal landing sites at Daiquiri and Siboney, following a route through the jungle toward Santiago. Despite their shortcomings, including poor training, a lack of experience, and unfamiliarity with the Cuban landscape, the U.S. soldiers fought hard against the Spanish. The major land action began in June and continued for several weeks.

A significant engagement took place on San Juan and Kettle Hill. The larger force advanced on Spanish entrenched positions at San Juan, while a secondary force, including the Rough Riders (who advanced not on horseback, but on foot, since they had reached Cuba without their mounts) and a pair of veteran black regiments, stormed up Kettle Hill. One of these regiments was the 10th Cavalry, commanded by a young white lieutenant and West Point graduate from Missouri, named John "Blackjack" Pershing. Pershing was destined to command all U.S. forces in World War I, but he first made his name during the advance up Kettle Hill, where his superior, Captain George Ayres, noticed him giving orders under fire while remaining, in the officer's words, notes historian Gene Smith, "as cool as a bowl of cracked ice."

As for Roosevelt, he moved up Kettle Hill on horseback and took a shot at a Spanish soldier whom he saw double up, later writing in his autobiography, "neatly as a jackrabbit." The former President later noted that he "would rather have led that charge than served three terms in the U.S. Senate."

DESTRUCTION OF THE SPANISH FLEET

These and other battles brought the U.S. victories, but they came at a heavy cost. Almost one out of every 10 Americans involved was either killed or wounded. The mid-summer temperatures hovered above 100° Farenheit (30° Centigrade), forcing the soldiers to fight the heat, as well as poor food, some of it spoiled and rotten. Disease plagued the men, and soon many were dying of malaria, yellow fever, and dysentery. Despite the problems, the Americans pushed on.

By nightfall on July 1, U.S. forces were entrenched in the hills overlooking Santiago. The Spanish governor of Cuba, Ramon Blanco y Erenas, ordered the Spanish fleet's commander, Admiral Cervera, to steam his ships out of harm's way and make a break for open waters. Cervera reluctantly obeyed. At dawn on July 3, a cloudy day, the ships emerged into the face of the waiting U.S. fleet, whose ships outnumbered the Spanish four to one. Four first-class U.S. battleships, two cruisers, and a variety of smaller vessels were directly in the path of the Spanish ships, having taken up positions in a half-circle blocking the harbor. Cervera's ships were lined up single file. One of the newest of the U.S. battleships, the *Oregon,* fired the first shot against the Spanish fleet, and soon the harbor was covered with a thick black smoke cloud, making visibility difficult for everyone.

BETWEEN TWO OCEANS

Following the Spanish–American War, the United States took over the Philippines, Puerto Rico, and Guam in the Pacific Ocean. The war spurred on the idea of building the Panama Canal linking the Pacific and Atlantic Oceans. The canal would enable U.S. ships of all kinds to move speedily across the globe. It would reduce the sea route from San Francisco to New York from 13,000 miles (20,900 km) to 5,200 miles (8,370 km).

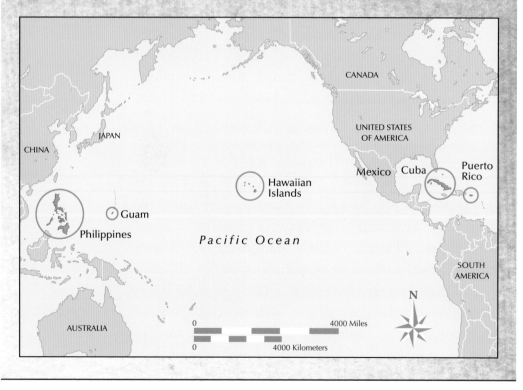

Outnumbered and outgunned, the Spanish fleet was doomed. One sailor on the *Oregon* described the battle as "a big turkey shoot." The Spanish vessels received heavy shelling, and fires broke out across their decks. In an attempt to escape death or capture, many Spanish crewmen jumped overboard. When the Spanish flagship, the *Maria Teresa,* seemed crippled by shelling, American sailors on the USS *Texas,* which had been built as a sister ship to the *Maine,* burst into a cheer. But the captain of the *Texas,* John W. Philip, put an immediate stop to their celebration, notes historian Richard F. Snow: "Don't cheer, boys," he ordered them. "Those poor devils are dying!"

The battle lasted only a few hours. The entire Spanish fleet in Cuba was destroyed, and some 500 Spanish sailors were killed. By comparison, no U.S. ship was seriously damaged and only one American died. This decisive battle effectively ended Spanish hopes of winning the war. Within two weeks, Spanish General Jose Torel surrendered to General William Rufus Shafter.

AMERICA BECOMES A COLONIAL POWER

The Spanish–American War was one of the shortest wars in U.S. history. The U.S. ambassador to Great Britain, John Hay, afterward referred to the conflict, notes historian Allen Weinstein, as "a splendid little war." Through four months of sporadic fighting, including sea battles, the United States suffered fewer than 500 battle-related deaths, just twice the number of men killed onboard the *Maine.* However, disease and poor sanitation killed close to 5,500 men.

Yet, despite the brevity of the war and the relatively limited loss of American lives, the Spanish–American War brought significant change to America. The war helped to improve relations between the North and South, still strained after the Civil War that had ended over 30 years before. It also brought the United States an extensive empire of overseas holdings. Under the Treaty of Paris, signed with the Spanish on December 10, 1898, Spain ceded control of Puerto Rico, Guam (a Pacific island), and the Philippines to the United States. Spain also granted Cuba its independence. In turn, the United States paid the Spanish government $20 million. The United States would occupy the island until 1909, when the Republic of Cuba was created. The United States had entered a war to help the Spanish colony gain independence, but, when the war ended, the American republic found itself a colonial power.

At first President McKinley was hesitant to take possession of the Philippines. They were, after all, far removed from the direct sphere of influence of the United States. But in November 1899 the president explained his ultimate willingness to annex the distant Pacific islands, notes historian Weinstein: "There was nothing left for us to do, but to take them all, and to educate the Filipinos, and to uplift and civilize and Christianize them, and by God's grace do the very best we could by them as our fellow men for whom Christ also died." To McKinley, taking the Philippines was nothing short of God's will.

But holding the Philippines proved less than providential. The Filipinos, it seems, were no more ready to accept U.S. dominance than they had been to accept Spanish rule. For three years, 70,000 U.S. troops fought in the islands, at a cost of $175 million, with a casualty list as high as that of the war with Spain. In 1902 the United States subdued the Filipinos, but at a cost of 4,300 American and between 50 and 200,000 Filipino lives. At least some of the spoils of the Spanish–American War proved bitter fruit, indeed.

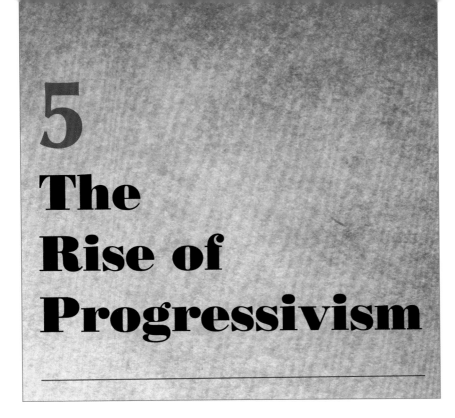

5

The Rise of Progressivism

In 1897 William McKinley took office as the nation's 24th president. Times being what they seemed, he and a Congress full of conservative Republicans had a clear road before them. The depression that had crippled the nation's economy between 1893 and 1896 had ended. Congress soon passed even higher trade barriers—including the Dingley Tariff, which elevated tariff rates to a new 57 percent high— to protect domestic industry. Farm prices went up, due to greater demand from Europe, where poor harvests caused grain shortages. Support for those fervent Populists melted away, the party collapsing, along with other reform groups. The nation rallied in support of the beleaguered Cubans to spread, they thought, democracy overseas, just as U.S. goods were finding markets around the world. America's season in the sun seemed to have returned, and many across the country were free to pursue their own prosperity and wave the flag of American patriotic pride.

THE PROGRESSIVE MOVEMENT

However, by the turn of the century, many middle-class Americans were seeing dangers in the road ahead. They felt America was a great nation, but one that still had flaws, gaps in opportunity, and where many people lived in poverty. They saw the great industrial giants wielding too much economic power over the country, as trusts limited competition. They saw political corruption at every turn, from their local city governments to the halls of Congress. Soon, various reform interests found one another and launched a political movement that historians have since labeled "Progressivism."

Just who were these "Progressives" and what did they want to accomplish? First, they were not generally doomsayers. They did not believe the collapse of U.S. society was close at hand. They were typically highly patriotic, nationalistic people who were generally optimistic about the country's capacity to fix its national problems and direct a positive program of change for the future. Patriotism and reform walked hand in hand with many Progressives, who believed that a decent society for all the nation's people could come about through gradual reform, rather than through barn-burning revolutionary steps.

Some motivations for the Progressives were fairly common. Many believed it was their Christian responsibility, a part of their personal moral framework, to support reform in America. This "social gospel" led Progressives to pursue such admirable goals as ending poverty, fighting injustice and unregulated industrial power, and campaigning for honest government officials. They also sought to preserve the nation's natural resources, seeing themselves as caretakers of God's creation.

One important aspect of the Progressive movement was a new found reliance on "experts"—well educated, highly trained, social and political scientists—who could approach the nation's problems with knowledge and expertise. The reformers sought the establishment of legislative investigating bodies and expert advisers, sometimes called "brain trusts," to work out overall solutions to help city and state governments battle corruption and bring about reform. They also supported non-partisan commissions or councils to bypass the power of the political bosses and machines that had maintained a stranglehold on urban politics for too many decades. By 1914 at least 400 U.S. cities had established some form of independent commission to operate their urban governments. This number did not include the nation's largest cities, however, where political bosses clung to their power.

The Muckrakers

A tool in the grab bag of tactics used by the Progressives was the publicizing of social problems to raise popular awareness. A number of writers wrote exposés on a wide variety of social ills. They came to be known as "muckrakers." Theodore Roosevelt applied the term first during a 1906 speech in which he praised those who exposed the nation's problems, while criticizing those who simply raised issues without providing solutions.

One of the leading Progressive magazine publishers was S. S. McClure. He hired several good writers who could turn a story with a journalistic hand for a wide audience. Among them were Ida Tarbell, Ray Stannard Baker, and Lincoln Steffens. Tarbell wrote an explosive series of articles for exposing the abusive business tactics of the Standard Oil Company. Lincoln Steffens wrote about the corrupt city political machines. Writer David Graham Phillips wrote on the high level of corruption taking place in the U.S. Senate. His series, *The Treason of the Senate*, helped bring about the passage of the Seventeenth Amendment to the Constitution,

Thanks to the Brooklyn Bridge built in 1883, which connected Manhattan and Brooklyn, Coney Island became a popular destination for day-trippers from New York City. Visitors could spend the day at the beach, go horse racing, or visit the amusement park.

which established the direct election of U.S. senators, rather than having them selected by state legislators.

One of the most widely read muckrakers was Upton Sinclair, whose 1906 novel, *The Jungle*, exposed the filthy conditions then found in U.S. meat-packing plants. Americans were disgusted when they read Sinclair's passages describing plants where, "a man could run his hand over these piles of meat and sweep off handfuls of the dried dung of rats." One of Sinclair's most high-profile readers, President Theodore Roosevelt, was inspired by the book to push through Congress the Meat Inspection Act and the Pure Food and Drug Act, which required government regulation of the country's food manufacturers.

REFORM BY GOVERNMENT

During the 1890s reformers gained control of a number of city governments and began ordering slum renewal and improvements in factory conditions. In New York City the corrupt Tammany Hall machine—the political organization that had run the city's Democrat politics for decades through a non-elected "boss" who held power by peddling influence—was now thrown out in 1901. The reform Mayor, Seth Low, worked alongside reformers to create tighter housing laws, provide health services to the poor, and establish such green spaces as parks and playgrounds.

Several states elected Progressive governors, including Robert LaFollette in Wisconsin, Charles Evans Hughes in New York, and Woodrow Wilson in New Jersey. These governors and others pushed for greater regulation of the railroads, public utilities, and of industries doing business within their respective states. State legislators also joined the bandwagon of reform, passing a variety of laws between 1900 and 1920. Maryland adopted the first state workmen's compensation law in 1902. The following year Oregon passed a law limiting the number of hours a day women could be required to work in industry to 10. Massachusetts passed the first minimum wage law in 1912, which only applied to women and children, since they were usually paid less than men.

THE TRIANGLE FACTORY FIRE

During the Progressive Movement countless reform laws were passed across the country to create safer working and living environments, limit child labor, and remedy a host of other social and economic ills. One particular tragedy convinced Americans of the need for such regulatory efforts on the part of government. This was the Triangle Shirtwaist Company Fire of 1911.

The company was housed on the seventh, eighth, and ninth floors of the 10-story Asch Building in New York City. There, garment workers, including hundreds of women and young girls, worked an average of 54 hours in a six-day week, Monday through Saturday. The Triangle garment shop was similar to hundreds of other shops around the city, employing tens of thousands of female workers.

On March 25 a fire broke out in the building, immediately trapping hundreds of people. The workers had never participated in a fire drill, so no one knew what to do. The eighth floor only had one exit door, which was kept locked by management to make certain that none of the women carried out fabric pieces.

No safety measures had been implemented in the building at all. There was just one fire escape for the entire building, but it only went down to the second floor. The three floors that housed the Triangle Factory had access to only two narrow staircases. The only other way out was by two small service elevators, large enough to carry just seven or eight people.

The shop was simply a fire trap, notes historian Allen Weinstein: "piles of cloth, tissue paper, rags, and cuttings covered the company's tables, shelves, and floors. The floors and machines were soaked with oil, and barrels of machine oil lined the walls."

On a national level, some of the greatest and most far-reaching changes came with the passage of new amendments to the U.S. Constitution. In 1913 the Progressives won two important constitutional victories with the passage of the

As fire spread through the building the workers panicked, desperate to find a way out. Hundreds of people became jammed together on the narrow staircases. Some reached the two freight elevators, but other workers jumped into the elevator shafts onto the tops of the elevators. The elevators stopped working after so many bodies crammed the elevator shaft. Death soon found its way to the street itself, with girls leaping out of upper story windows.

Firefighters soon arrived, and within 15 minutes, had the flames under control. But the fire had burned so quickly that firefighters found the burned corpses of 100 employees, many of them Jewish workers, and all but 21 of them women. Nearly a dozen were so badly burned by the fire that they were never identified. On the floor of the factory, workers would later find 14 engagement rings.

In the aftermath of this tragedy citizens in New York City were outraged. Pressure came to bear on the politicians, who began righting as many wrongs as they could. The state legislature established the New York Factory Investigating Commission in June 1911, to examine working conditions in factories.

Between 1911 and 1915 the New York state legislature saw the introduction of more than 60 bills concerning working conditions, and passed 56 of them. New laws created a Bureau of Fire Prevention; compulsory fire drills at work places; the installation of sprinklers in factories; more factory inspectors; a statewide working week of 54 hours for men as well as women; minimum wages for women and children; a ban on smoking in factories, and a host of other measures.

The Triangle Shirtwaist Company Fire had caused many people in New York to wake up to the horrible working conditions that its unprotected laborers had struggled under for many years, all in the name of decency and Progressivism.

Sixteenth Amendment, which established a federal income tax, and the Seventeenth Amendment, which brought about a reform hawked by the Populists more than a decade earlier—direct election of U.S. senators. Other amendments followed. As part of the moral streak imbedded in Progressivism, the Eighteenth Amendment, which prohibited alcohol, was ratified by the states in January 1919.

One further amendment was ratified in 1920 after a long campaign of support. The Nineteenth Amendment granted women across the country the right to vote. Between 1914 and 1919 women's rights advocates marched in the streets in support of female suffrage. Prior to World War I (1914–18) only 11 states allowed women to vote. Congress passed the amendment in June 1919 and ratification followed 14 months later.

The U.S. Supreme Court also weighed in on the Progressive agenda. In the 1905 decision *Lochner v. New York*, the Court struck down a law that required a 10-hour day for workers, as it violated the workers' "liberty of contract," since they had to accept the number of hours set by the law. Three years later the Court upheld a law limiting female workers to 10 hours a day. The case, *Muller v. Oregon,* was based on evidence presented that argued longer hours were detrimental to the health and moral fiber of women. In 1917 *Bunting v. Oregon* established a 10-hour work day for both men and women.

PROGRESSIVES IN THE WHITE HOUSE

William McKinley, a conservative Republican president, had little opportunity to show his support for the budding Progressive movement as he was assassinated in 1901. With McKinley's death, New Yorker Theodore Roosevelt was thrust onto the national stage as the nation's chief executive. At first Roosevelt promised to pursue McKinley's policies, which had not been particularly progressive. For nearly eight years, however, Theodore Roosevelt would not only advance the Progressive agenda, he would redefine the role of a U.S. president. Roosevelt's domestic program, which became known as his "Square Deal," was primarily aimed at helping middle-class citizens and included conservation measures, anti-monopoly legislation, trust busting, and other progressive legislation.

Underlying Roosevelt's actions and policies concerning Progressivism were certain firm beliefs he shared with his fellow reformers. Among them was the belief that the government should be used as the only viable instrument of restraint against unregulated business interests. Armed with that philosophy, he supported and saw passage by Congress of several important Progressive measures, including the Elkins Act of 1903, which banned railroads from giving rebates to their large corporate customers, and the Hepburn Act of 1906, which provided additional teeth for the Interstate Commerce Commission to regulate the country's railroad companies.

Teddy the Trust Buster

One of the most significant and bold steps taken by Roosevelt to advance the Progressive agenda was to tackle some of the nation's larger corporate trusts. Despite earlier attempts to rein in monopolies and business trusts, such as the Interstate Commerce Commission (ICC) and the Sherman Antitrust Act, trusts remained a reality. Although a hard-core capitalist, Roosevelt began to speak out against the nation's business tycoons and corporate heads, whom he perceived were not acting in the best interests of the people.

Initially Roosevelt tried to bring trusts under control through regulation, asking Congress to pass laws that would authorize the licensing of corporations by the federal government and require companies to disclose their earnings and profits. But conservatives in Congress generally blocked most of these efforts. Not to be outdone, Roosevelt tried another tack. He would take on the trusts himself, armed with the power and authority of the Sherman Antitrust Act.

In 1902 Roosevelt's first target was a consolidated railroad conglomerate, the Northern Securities Company, which Wall Street mogul J. Pierpont Morgan had helped create in 1901. By 1904 the President had won his case, with the Supreme Court declaring that the merger of multiple rail lines that had formed Northern Securities had been illegal, and ordering the company to be broken up. This victory only marked the beginning of Roosevelt's "trust busting" campaign. Roosevelt remained committed to breaking up trusts throughout his presidency, with his justice department filing a total of 44 antitrust suits against large business combinations. Some trusts, however, the President refused to file against, such as those he thought were acting responsibly toward citizens.

Meanwhile Roosevelt's and Morgan's paths crossed over another business-related issue. In 1902 the president, facing a coal strike with winter approaching, used his authority to force an agreement between the coal miners and coal company officials. J. Pierpont Morgan helped the President by forcing coal company executives to accept a settlement that favored the coal miners. Never before had a U.S. president intervened in a labor dispute by siding with the striking workers.

A Conservationist President

As an avid hunter and fanatical outdoorsman, Roosevelt was concerned about the nation's natural resources. He felt it was important to educate Americans about land management and environmental protection. In 1902 his Newlands Act was passed, which authorized federal monies for the building of dams and water reclamation projects across the West. Five years later he signed an executive order converting 172 million acres (70 million ha) of western forestland into national reserves, which would not be open to private sale or use, using the Forest Reserve Act of 1891 as his justification. He also authorized the first federal bird preserve in America

Theodore Roosevelt, shown here on horseback at Yellowstone Park in 1903, was a fan of what he called "the strenuous life" and practised many sports. His love of outdoor pursuits inspired him to set up bird reserves and national parks when president.

and established a network of 55 bird reserves and national game preserves for wildlife. He approved five new national parks and withdrew from private purchase lands rich in natural resources. In 1908 he invited a group of conservation experts to a conference at the White House to discuss future policies intended to protect America's natural resources.

By the time Theodore Roosevelt left the White House in 1909 (having been elected in his own right as president in 1904) he had advanced the agenda of the Progressive Party more than any single individual in the country. As he neared the end of his second term, Roosevelt admitted, historian Tindall notes: "I have had a great time as president."

TAFT AS A PROGRESSIVE

In 1908 Roosevelt was so popular as president that he was able to virtually handpick his successor, choosing his secretary of war, William Howard Taft. Taft entered office in March 1909. He carried out additional actions in support of Progressivism, even if he was more conservative than Roosevelt. Taft supported passage of the Sixteenth and Seventeenth Amendments. His justice department also filed nearly twice as many anti-trust suits (80) as Roosevelt's, and did so in half as many years. His administration worked with Congress on other Progressive legislation, including establishing the eight-hour working day for government workers, extending the ICC's authority to include communications systems that crossed state lines, and an increase in taxes on corporate profits.

Still, Taft did not gain the reputation with the public as a trust-buster that Roosevelt did, in part because Taft did not project himself out to the public, whereas Roosevelt had constantly tried to place himself in the public eye. Eventually, Taft ran into trouble with a holdover of Roosevelt's administration, Foresty Chief Gifford Pinchot. Taft was forced to fire Pinchot after the Forestry Chief criticized Pinchot publicly for allowing private companies to tap coal and water power sites on federal land in Alaska. When Roosevelt learned of Taft's move against one of his former cabinet members, the former president was furious, and regretful that he had ever supported his war secretary for president. By 1910 Roosevelt was campaigning in the press against Taft, stating that his former friend had "sold the Square Deal down the river."

THE ELECTION OF 1912

In the 1912 election, Roosevelt ran against the president. He courted the Republican nomination, but did not receive it, as Old Guard Republicans chose to stick with Taft. This led Roosevelt to run as a third party candidate, even though the old line Progressive Robert LaFollette of Wisconsin did not believe Roosevelt to have been a strong enough supporter of Progressive reform. In the fall of 1912 the Progressive Party nominated Roosevelt as their candidate. One sidelight to Roosevelt's campaign was an attempt made on his life. In October, in Milwaukee, the former president was shot at close range by a gunman. Roosevelt was wounded in the chest, but delivered his scheduled speech that evening before having the bullet removed.

The election campaign was a field day for Progressivism. The Progressive Party platform included such reforms as tighter government regulation of giant industries, national presidential primaries, women's suffrage, and the old Populist political reforms from 1896—the initiative and the referendum—and the recall. Progressives also supported the prohibition of child labor, minimum wages for women, workmen's compensation, and banking and currency reforms.

The Republicans ran on a moderate platform, which included regulation of the trusts, as well as banking and currency reform, while the Democrats nominated a moderate reformer, Governor Woodrow Wilson of New Jersey. The Democrat party platform supported collective bargaining for labor unions, banking reform, and the breaking up of giant corporate trusts, not just their regulation. Governor Wilson called the party's program the New Freedom. A fourth candidate, socialist Eugene V. Debs, ran on the most radicalized platform, one that called for the nationalization of all U.S. resources and industry.

With the Republicans split between Roosevelt and Taft, Wilson pulled out a victory, gaining 6.3 million votes to Roosevelt's 4.1 and Taft's 3.5 million. As for the socialist Debs, he received almost 1 million votes. Electorally, Wilson gained 435 votes to Roosevelt's 88 and Taft's 8. Woodrow Wilson became only the second Democrat president to be elected since James Buchanan in 1856, the first having been Grover Cleveland.

WILSON'S PROGRESSIVISM

During his first term, the Democrat president set out to implement his progressive agenda. He did not try to break up trusts, as Roosevelt and Taft had, but pushed for greater regulation of the giant corporate entities. To that end, Congress enacted the Federal Trade Commission Act of 1914, which established a bipartisan body to overview and supervise industrial corporations and prevent unfair competitive practices in interstate commerce. Also, the Clayton Antitrust Act of 1914 was passed, which gave more teeth to the old 1890 Sherman Antitrust Act by specifying what business practices violated antitrust laws.

Other reforms that became reality during Wilson's first term included the Federal Reserve Act, which was passed in December 1913. The nation had struggled without a federal banking system for more than 75 years, since the days when

President Jackson vetoed the rechartering of the Second Bank of the United States during the 1830s. This new legislation created the federal reserve system, with 12 regionally serving federal reserve banks. Each was to see to member banks in their various geographic districts. Federal reserve banks were authorized to issue paper currency, supervise bank credit, and control other banking practices. Passage of the act was long overdue.

Other progressive acts passed during Wilson's first term included the Federal Farm Loan Act (1916), which aided farmers and other agriculturalists by making more credit available. The Adamson Act, also passed in 1916, established the eight-hour working day for workers involved in interstate commerce and the railroad industry. The Kern–McGillicuddy Act (1916) created a workmen's compensation program for federal employees. The Keating–Owen Act (1916) banned the interstate shipment of consumer goods and other products manufactured using child labor under the age of 14, but that law was declared unconstitutional two years later. A boon to the nation's transportation needs took shape in the Federal Highways Act of 1916, which authorized matching funds to state governments for highway construction. Five years later, the act was renewed. These new laws marked the beginning of the system of numbered U.S. highways.

By 1916 Wilson had continued the Progressive agenda considerably, earning him enough presidential credit to facilitate his reelection. Since the summer of 1914 Europe had been blazing with the fires of a great world war, and during the election the Democrats made frequent use of the campaign slogan: "He Kept Us Out of War." Despite pressures abroad and at home, Wilson had managed to steer the country clear of the conflict. But just as Wilson launched into his second term, the war finally caught up with him.

6

A New Foreign Policy

The United States began taking a new approach to international diplomacy during the early decades of the twentieth century, an approach that would set the nation on a course of direct involvement with other countries through a foreign policy as aggressive as any ever pursued by America's leaders.

While the United States had typically maintained a low-key, understated set of foreign policies that could be called anything but aggressive, after 1900 Presidents Roosevelt, Taft, and Wilson each made their own contributions to "progressive diplomacy," which usually involved government support of the nation's commercial interests and their expansion overseas by facilitating trade treaties. To back up an increased U.S. trade presence, as well as a higher level of political involvement in other countries, America's leaders were more prepared to back up their diplomatic moves with a growing military presence.

Just as Progressivism emphasized social change based on a moral agenda, so the new U.S. foreign policy was based on moral leadership, plus an emphasis on encouraging ordered foreign governments, and a belief that God had chosen the United States to take a greater role in international affairs. That "moral" approach sometimes amounted to little more than an assumed moral superiority on the part of the United States, which other countries sometimes had a hard time accepting. But, by the opening of World War I in 1914, America had already gained a new level of status as one of the world's leading powers.

"SPEAK SOFTLY"

As president, Theodore Roosevelt enjoyed taking a "hands on," even aggressive, approach to U.S. foreign policy. He believed America was a superior country with its Protestant, Anglo-Saxon culture, so much so that he thought those values should be extended to other countries. He believed in a strong U.S. military, one that could protect and even help increase America's international economic role.

Roosevelt is often remembered for a phrase he used to describe his approach to U.S. foreign policy, a West African proverb that stated: "Speak softly and carry a big stick, and you will go far." The President did not hesitate to wield that "big stick" by involving America in several situations in the Caribbean region. None would have a greater impact than the role he played in forcing the construction of a canal across the Central American Isthmus of Panama to provide a direct link between the Atlantic and Pacific Oceans.

THE PANAMA CANAL

The President believed that a canal across Panama was his top priority. In 1903 he tried to negotiate an agreement with the South American nation of Columbia, which had control of Panama at that time, but the Columbian Senate rejected a U.S. deal to construct a canal. Not to be outdone, Roosevelt soon intervened, relying on a French engineer and agent for the New Panama Canal Company, Philippe Bunau-Varilla.

THE PANAMA CANAL BY NUMBERS

When the Panama Canal opened for business in 1914 it signaled the completion of one of the greatest construction projects in history. For starters, 262 million cubic yds (200 cu m) of earth and rock were removed in constructing the canal.

The cost of the project was $352 million—a staggering sum in its day. Add in the money spent by a French canal company before the Americans arrived, and the bill comes in at approximately $639 million.

But the cost of building the canal can be calculated in a different way—the cost in lives. According to U.S. records, which begin in 1904, 5,609 workers died from disease and accidents. Again, add the number of French lives lost, and the number swells to nearly 25,000. This represents about one worker lost for every 10 ft (3 m) that the building work progressed across the Canal Zone.

But there are other significant statistics. The Panama Canal was completed ahead of schedule by six months, despite constant delays caused by landslides. The project, despite its high price tag, was completed under budget, by about $23 million. The U.S. effort was completed without scandal, bribes, kickbacks, or corruption, and no company was ever accused of having made excessive profits.

Traffic passing through the canal was light during the years of World War I, averaging about 2,000 ships annually. But within 10 years of opening, about 5,000 ships were being taken through the canal each year. Since 1960 the Panama Canal has handled from 12,000 to 15,000 ships annually, As many as 50 ships transit the canal each day, and traffic passes through 24 hours a day. The length of the average transit is about eight hours.

(The French had spent years trying to construct a canal across the Isthmus, an effort that had failed dramatically.)

Roosevelt informed Bunau-Varilla that he was sending warships to Panama. The first, the USS *Nashville*, arrived in Colon Harbor on November 3, 1903. Almost immediately the Columbian province of Panama started a revolution, declaring itself independent of Columbian control. Immediately, Roosevelt recognized the Republic of Panama.

Within two weeks Bunau-Varilla was serving as the de facto minister from Panama. He signed a treaty granting the United States complete sovereignty over a 10-mile (16-km) wide stretch of Panama extending across the country. In exchange, U.S. officials supported Panamanian independence, made a down payment of $10 million, and agreed to pay an additional $250,000 annually in perpetuity. Roosevelt made no bones about what he had done by supporting Panama's revolution against Columbia. In his typical, plain-spoken manner, he later bragged, notes historian David McCullough: "I took Panama."

Roosevelt then set out to build a canal across Panama. It became a Herculean project, a wonder of modern engineering methods. The project also provided the United States with great strategic and commercial advantages. Building the canal took nearly a decade, with thousands of laborers from dozens of countries, mostly throughout the Caribbean.

The Panama Canal cost $639 million to construct and remains an engineering marvel even today, with an elaborate lock system that continues to accommodate the vast majority of modern-day ships. But when the canal opened for business in 1914, its completion was overshadowed in the world's newspapers by the opening engagements of the World War I.

While the canal was a boon to international trade, allowing ships to cut thousands of miles off the journey from the

Atlantic to the Pacific by eliminating the necessity of sailing around South America, it was also of strategic importance to the United States. Theodore Roosevelt's second secretary of state, Elihu Root, said in 1905, years before the canal's completion, notes historian Walter LeFeber: "The inevitable effect of our building the Canal must be to require us to police the surrounding premises." On that score, Root was speaking for President Roosevelt, who also believed in the necessity of a greater U.S. role in monitoring the Western Hemisphere.

THE ROOSEVELT COROLLARY

One of the president's great concerns was the ongoing potential for European powers to intervene in the affairs of nations in the New World, especially if the United States did not exert its presence to discourage them. Early in the nineteenth century, President James Monroe had declared that nations of the Western Hemisphere were no longer to be considered subject for European colonization. But the latter years of that same century witnessed a great scramble for European colonies in Africa and Asia. Latin America also seemed a natural target for expanding European powers.

Therefore in 1904, just as construction on the Panama Canal had begun, Roosevelt announced his addition to the 80-year-old Monroe Doctrine, known as the Roosevelt Corollary. The President declared, notes historian Richard Heffner: "Chronic Wrongdoing, or an impotence which results in a general loosening of the ties of civilized society" would compel the United States to engage in "the exercise of an international police power" throughout the Western Hemisphere. Roosevelt's meaning: If any nation put itself in a position of vulnerability due to poor leadership, the United States would intervene in their affairs and straighten that nation out to the satisfaction of the American republic.

Roosevelt did not wait long to enforce his corollary. In 1905, the Caribbean island of the Dominican Republic was behind in its debt payments to European creditors. To deter European military intervention in the island nation, the

The Panama Canal consists of a number of channels and artificial lakes, along with three sets of gigantic locks. This photograph, taken around 1910 when the canal was still under construction, shows a ship in one of the locks, near the Atlantic end of the canal.

President stepped in instead. With agreement from the Caribbean nation's leaders, the United States was given permission to install and protect a customs collector, who would siphon some of the island's trade revenues to make debt payments to European bankers. The crisis was averted, for the time being, but the Roosevelt Corollary would be used a decade later to justify U.S. military intervention into the Dominican Republic, with U.S. troops remaining on the island between 1916 and 1924.

THE RUSSO–JAPANESE WAR OF 1904

While Roosevelt was asserting the authority and power of the United States on its Latin American neighbors, war broke out half way across the globe. In 1904 two mighty Asian powers—Japan and Russia—opened hostilities. This worried Roosevelt. His immediate concern was that the war would jeopardize America's overall foreign policy in Asia, known as the "Open Door."

This policy had been cobbled together by William McKinley's secretary of state, John Hay, in 1899. (Hay continued to serve Roosevelt as secretary of state after McKinley's death.) Japan and various western European powers had already forced open China to their economic markets. By the time the United States sought to open its own doors in Asia's largest state, much of China's market had already been gobbled up. Hay, however, had managed to secure guarantees for equal access for U.S. companies and commercial ventures in China. Ultimately Hay, through a series of diplomatic approaches, was able to put together his Open Door approach, which pried open China, giving all nations equal access to her current markets and to developing future markets.

With war now breaking out between Japan and Russia, the delicate balance of power in Asia appeared in question, threatening U.S. business interests in the region. Roosevelt became very alarmed as Japan dealt several serious blows against the Russians. If Japan emerged as the dominant power in Asia, America's hold over the Philippines might be jeopardized.

Roosevelt the Peace Maker

The Japanese opened the war with a surprise attack on the Russian fleet on February 8, 1904, which destroyed many ships. Then they marched into Korea and pushed the Russians inland, back to Manchuria. But then the war devolved into a virtual stalemate, with neither side able to defeat the other ultimately. Both sides feared their war might drag on endlessly, draining manpower.

Roosevelt then offered to broker a conclusion to the war, and invited representatives from both sides to come to the United States to a peace conference held at Portsmouth, New Hampshire. In 1905 peace was concluded through the Treaty of Portsmouth, with Japan gaining Russia's recognition of its new dominance over Korea and its economic control over Manchuria, even as Japanese troops were withdrawn. Japan would later annex Korea in 1910. For his efforts, President Roosevelt received the Nobel Peace Prize in 1906.

Tension with Japan

Not all was well, however, between the United States and Japan. Repeatedly, anti-Japanese racism had reared its head in the United States, typically in California, where the San Francisco school board ordered Asian students, including Japanese, Chinese, and Korean, to be segregated from white students. Roosevelt had dispatched his secretary of war, William Howard Taft, to Tokyo even as the Portsmouth negotiations were taking place. Taft and the Japanese foreign minister managed to hammer out the Taft–Katsura Agreement during the summer of 1905. Under this agreement, the

United States agreed to Japanese control of Korea as Japan agreed not to make any moves against the Philippines. Back in the States, Roosevelt convinced the San Francisco school board to end segregation of Japanese students in the city's school system. One motivation for the policy change in San Francisco was the threat by Japan to seriously curtail issuing passports to U.S. citizens.

Intent on making certain that the Japanese did not interpret any U.S. moves or agreements as a sign of weakness, Roosevelt began building up the navy. In 1908, his last full year in office, he dispatched U.S. warships to pay a friendly call on Japan, so the Japanese could see for themselves the level of power represented by America's newest naval vessels. The ships were received by thousands of Japanese school children, who waved U.S. flags and sang "The Star Spangled Banner" in English.

This was part of a worldwide effort by Roosevelt to display the new fleet—called the "Great White Fleet" because U.S. warships at that time were painted in a light, nearly white color—around the world. The U.S. Navy, by 1907, was one of the largest in the world, second only to Great Britain. The ships were sent across the Pacific, through the Suez Canal, and into the Mediterranean, before sailing back home across the Atlantic in 1909. By then Roosevelt had left office and President Taft was at the helm.

TAFT AND DOLLAR DIPLOMACY

When Taft entered the presidency, he came with more direct foreign policy experience than Roosevelt had brought to the office. He had overseen, as secretary of war, the construction of the Panama Canal and had earlier served as governor of the Philippines. Taft believed he could pursue a foreign policy that relied less on Roosevelt's militaristic "Big Stick" and used a more subtle approach. He and his secretary of state, a former corporate lawyer and Roosevelt's attorney general, Philander Knox, formulated a policy later called "Dollar Diplomacy" by their critics. The thinking behind the policy was that once the United States established trade and investment in a foreign nation, then political influence would naturally follow. In Taft's words, notes historian Robert M. Crunden, his foreign policy supported "active intervention to secure for our merchandise and our capitalists opportunity for profitable investment."

However, Taft's "Dollar Diplomacy" did not work out as well as he hoped. In the Caribbean and in Asia, his policy of "dollars rather than bullets" proved of limited value. U.S. investment did expand. In Central America, for example, U.S. businesses increased their investments from $41 million in 1908 to $93 million by 1914. (Taft was out of the White House by 1913.) Much of that capital went to the building of railroads on foreign soil, mining, and plantations. By 1913 the U.S. firm, United Fruit Company, owned approximately 160,000 acres (65,000 hectares) of land throughout the Caribbean.

But Taft then had to back up U.S. investment with U.S. military forces, as he dispatched naval ships and marines to intervene during disputes in Honduras and Nicaragua. In both instances U.S. military personnel were sent in to provide support for political groups in those countries that were committed to protect U.S. business interests. U.S. marines maintained a presence in Nicaragua until 1933. Taft's dollars had to be backed up by bullets.

In Asia Taft faced other problems with his policy. He and Knox pushed for a higher level of investment for U.S. businesses in China, even gaining U.S. bankers a role in the consortium of European bankers backing the construction of a huge railroad, the Hu-Kuang Railway in central and southern China. But Taft misstepped when he finagled a large international loan for the Chinese government, one that would allow China to purchase all the foreign railroads operating on its soil. Japan and Russia had both fought wars to plant their railroad interests in Manchuria, so when they learned of this move, they resisted. Taft's plan, intended to gain a greater U.S. relationship with the Chinese Nationalists who revolted in 1911 against the ruling Manchu Dynasaty, led Japan to sign a treaty with Russia, reestablishing friendly relations, and created a united wall against U.S. policy in China. Taft's "Open Door" in Asia began closing, as Japan and the United States drifted apart. Over the following 30 years, these two countries slipped further into opposing roles, which ultimately lead to a clash of arms during World War II.

PRESIDENT WILSON'S "MORALISM"

No sooner had President Woodrow Wilson taken the office in the spring of 1913, than he made an observation that was to prove prophetic, notes historian Eileen Welsome: "It would be the irony of fate if my administration had to deal chiefly with foreign affairs."

Wilson had made his name in politics through his Progressive governorship of New Jersey. He had absolutely no foreign policy experience, but set out to base his diplomacy on a moral view of the world and a faith in U.S. democracy. Wilson established his policies on his belief that U.S. economic expansion, supported by democratic idealism and Christianity, represented a civilizing influence in the modern world of the twentieth century. He thought the "Open Door" policy to be a good one, even as he believed that tariffs were nothing more than barriers to trade. While the Presbyterian Woodrow Wilson tried to apply his amalgamation of economic expansionism, democracy, and Christian morals to his foreign policy, things did not always work out ideally for him or for the United States.

TROUBLE SOUTH OF THE BORDER

During Wilson's first term as president one of his biggest foreign policy headaches was Mexico. In 1911 Mexican revolutionaries overthrew the longtime, repressive Mexican dictator, Porfirio Diaz, replacing him with a popular leader named Francisco Madero, who promised democracy and economic reform for Mexican peasants. Madero remained in office from October 1911 until February 1913.

Although U.S. businesses with investments in Mexico were uncertain how Madero's presidency might affect them, Wilson supported Madero, whom he believed was a champion of democracy. (Wilson, of course, was only campaigning for the presidency during the period that Madero was in office.) But, just before Wilson took office, Madero was assassinated by his chief lieutenant, General Victoriano Huerta, whom historian William Weber Johnson refers to as a "bullet-headed [*mestizo*] Indian with weak eyes and a rumbling bass voice."

The Huerta Government

While other world powers, such as Great Britain and Japan, recognized the new Huerta government, Wilson would not. Madero had been murdered by Huerta supporters and Wilson could not sanction a government that came to power outside the rule of law. Meanwhile a Mexican opposition group, the Constitutionalists led by Venustiano Carranza, took up arms against Huerta. The U.S. president then put himself in the middle of the revolution by trying to work out a compromise between the two warring sides, but neither group was interested. By 1914 Carranza was able to buy guns from the United States, as Wilson tried to isolate Huerta by successfully persuading the British to drop their support of the Mexican dictator in exchange for U.S. promises to protect British business interests in Mexico.

But Huerta stubbornly remained as president. Then, in the spring of 1914, Wilson invaded Mexico, using the flimsy excuse that some American sailors had been arrested in Tampico by Mexican officials (they had, of course, for fighting in a Mexican cantina). U.S. forces bombed, then occupied the port of Veracruz, where Huerta was receiving arms shipments from Europe. Nineteen Americans and 126 Mexicans were killed, setting off a series of anti-American protests throughout Latin America. Some of those powers—Brazil, Argentina, and Chile—intervened, asking to mediate a solution. Wilson agreed to the request from the "ABC Powers," but Carranza soon managed to overthrow Huerta.

Ironically, Carranza did not consider Wilson to be a friend to Mexico. Rather, he spoke out against the U.S. president's recent show of military power on his country's soil. Wilson was left uncertain which direction to turn. For a while, he gave support to Francisco "Pancho" Villa, a former ally of Carranza's, who had helped to remove Huerta. Villa, dissatisfied with Carranza's leadership, turned on his former revolutionary comrade and continued to fight the Mexican government. By 1915 Villa had been defeated, and Wilson chose to recognize Carranza as the legitimate leader of Mexico.

The Hunt for Pancho Villa

This move by the U.S. leader left Pancho Villa bitter, feeling that he had been betrayed by the United States. In an attempt to try to provoke war between the United States and Mexico, Villa led several raids across the border into the American Southwest, where his men shot up border towns, such as Columbus, New Mexico, and killed several dozen Americans. (In earlier years, Villa had crossed the border at El Paso, Texas, but only to buy ice cream from his favorite ice cream parlor.)

Wilson was outraged, and dispatched General John "Blackjack" Pershing—a hero of the Spanish–American War whom President Roosevelt had advanced to the rank of general—along with 15,000 U.S. forces, to track down Villa in northern Mexico. For most of a year, Pershing's men scrambled across the desert lands of Sonora and Chihuahua,

General John J. Pershing (center) and Lieutenant George S. Patton (left) lead their troops across the Santa Maria River in Mexico in 1916, during their pursuit of the revolutionary leader Pancho Villa. They were never able to capture him.

moving 300 miles (480 km) deep into Mexican territory. Although war did not break out between the two countries, because at first Carranza okayed Pershing's punitive expedition into Mexico to capture Villa, the result was to further turn Villa into a folk hero, one who symbolized national resistance in Mexico. Supporters flocked to Villa's army—known as *villistas*—increasing his numbers from 500 men to 10,000 by the end of 1916.

Pershing was never able to find Villa and capture him. The Mexican *pistolero* managed to dodge U.S. forces, striking against them with hit-and-run tactics. Pershing, who had known from the outset that his mission would likely fail, complained that he felt, notes historian Gene Smith, his efforts were similar to finding "a rat in a cornfield." The frustrated general at one point even suggested the U.S. government should annex Chihuahua, and later called for the U.S. occupation of all of Mexico. Wilson actually drafted such a suggestion to present to Congress, but never made the request. Even his fellow Americans had decided that the Pershing expedition was a mistake.

A Way Out of Mexico

U.S. Army forces remained in Mexico from March 1916 to January 1917. Carranza finally tired of the U.S. presence, and war nearly broke out between Carranza's army and Pershing's men during the summer of 1916. Wilson became desperate for a way out of Mexico that would save U.S. integrity.

When an international commission suggested the removal of U.S. forces from Mexican soil, the president finally agreed, citing his concerns over events that were unfolding in Europe. Since the summer of 1914 Europe had been engulfed in a great war. Wilson used this as his pretext for leaving Mexico. He said, notes historian Jennifer D. Keene: "Germany is anxious to have us at war with Mexico, so that our minds and our energies will be taken off the great war across the sea." Pershing received his orders and, on February 5, 1917, he and his columns of now highly experienced field forces crossed the Mexican–American border at Columbus, New Mexico, as military bands played "When Johnny Comes Marching Home."

In reality, the war in Europe was of far greater importance than any continuing U.S. presence in Mexico. Wilson announced that he had no interest in interfering with Mexican sovereignty. Unfortunately, his actions had already planted the seeds of distrust and suspicion among the Mexican government and its people.

But Wilson had only begun to bear the burdens of international crisis. The war in Europe would soon engulf even the United States, and the nation's role as a major player in the arena of international affairs would be put to far greater tests than it had faced in the deserts of Sonora and Chihuahua, or indeed at any time during its previous 140-year history.

Chronology

1869 Knights of Labor founded

1870 New York City opens its first elevated railroad. John Rockefeller forms the Standard Oil Company of Ohio

1871 Fire destroys much of the city of Chicago

1872 Ulysses S. Grant elected president

1873 First cable cars in use in San Francisco

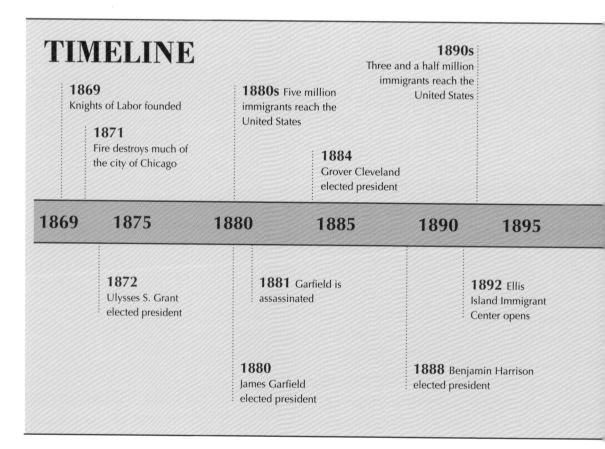

TIMELINE

1869
Knights of Labor founded

1871
Fire destroys much of the city of Chicago

1880s Five million immigrants reach the United States

1884
Grover Cleveland elected president

1890s
Three and a half million immigrants reach the United States

| 1869 | 1875 | 1880 | 1885 | 1890 | 1895 |

1872
Ulysses S. Grant elected president

1881 Garfield is assassinated

1892 Ellis Island Immigrant Center opens

1880
James Garfield elected president

1888 Benjamin Harrison elected president

1875 Congress passes Resumption Act

1876 Telephone is introduced at the Centennial Exposition in Philadelphia. Later that year, Thomas Alva Edison invents a practical incandescent light bulb. Rutherford B. Hayes elected president

1877 Edison patents the phonograph. Great Railroad Strike

1878 Congress passes the Bland–Allison Act

1880s Five million immigrants reach the United States

1880 James Garfield elected president

1881 Garfield is assassinated

1882 Congress passes act restricting Chinese immigration to the United States

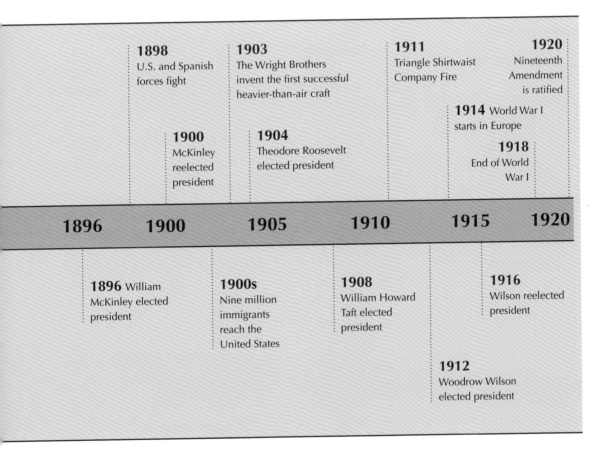

1898 U.S. and Spanish forces fight

1903 The Wright Brothers invent the first successful heavier-than-air craft

1911 Triangle Shirtwaist Company Fire

1920 Nineteenth Amendment is ratified

1900 McKinley reelected president

1904 Theodore Roosevelt elected president

1914 World War I starts in Europe

1918 End of World War I

1896   **1900**   **1905**   **1910**   **1915**   **1920**

1896 William McKinley elected president

1900s Nine million immigrants reach the United States

1908 William Howard Taft elected president

1916 Wilson reelected president

1912 Woodrow Wilson elected president

1883 Brooklyn Bridge, the nation's longest suspension
    bridge, opens. Pendleton Civil Service Act passes
1884 Grover Cleveland elected president
1885 First skyscraper utilizing an iron girder framework is
    built in Chicago
1886 Haymarket Riot in Chicago
1887 Federal Division of the Forestry is created. Cleveland
    vetoes Dependent Pension Bill. Interstate
    Commerce Act is passed
1888 First electric streetcars in use in Richmond, Virginia.
    George Eastman patents his Kodak camera.
    Benjamin Harrison elected president
1889–90 Six new states added to the Union: North and
    South Dakota, Montana, Wyoming, Washington,
    and Idaho
1890s Three and a half million immigrants reach the
    United States
1890 United Mine Workers union is organized. Congress
    passes the Dependent Pension Act, Sherman Silver
    Purchase Act, McKinley Tariff Act, and Sherman
    Antitrust Act
1891 Populist Party is founded
1892 Ellis Island Immigrant Center opens. U.S. Supreme
    Court orders the break of up Rockefeller's Standard
    Oil Company. J. Pierpont Morgan finances new
    company: General Electric. Homestead Strike takes
    place outside Pittsburgh. Grover Cleveland elected
    to a second, non-consecutive term as president
1893 United States falls into economic depression
1894 Pullman Strike
1895 Cuban Revolution starts
1896 William McKinley elected president
1898

February 9 DeLome Letter is published

February 15 The battleship USS *Maine* mysteriously explodes in Havana Harbor, Cuba

April 11 President McKinley requests war declaration against Spain. Congress makes this on April 25

May 1 Admiral Dewey defeats the Spanish fleet in Manila Bay, Philippines

July 1 U.S. and Spanish forces fight on San Juan and Kettle Hills

July 3 U.S. naval forces defeat Spanish fleet at Santiago, Cuba

December 10 Spain cedes control of Puerto Rico, Guam, and the Philippines to the United States

1898–1902 U.S. military fights Filipinos for control of the Philippines

1900s Nine million immigrants reach the United States

1900 McKinley reelected president

1901 J. Pierpont Morgan purchases Andrew Carnegie's steel interests. McKinley is assassinated in Buffalo

1902 Maryland adopts the first state workmen's compensation law. Roosevelt files suit against J. Pierpont Morgan's Northern Securities Company. Roosevelt's Newlands Act is passed by Congress

1903 The Wright Brothers invent the first successful heavier-than-air craft. Oregon passes a law limiting the number of hours women may work daily. Congress passes the Elkins Act. Roosevelt establishes the nation's first federal bird preserve. Roosevelt supports Panama's revolution against Columbia

1904 York City's first subway line is completed. Theodore Roosevelt elected president. Roosevelt establishes Bureau of Corporations. U.S. Supreme Court orders breakup of Northern Securities Company. Work on the Panama Canal starts

Chronology

1905 U.S. Supreme Court decision, *Lochner v. New York.* Roosevelt intervenes in the Dominican Republic. and brokers peace between Japan and Russia

1906 Congress subsequently passes the Pure Food and Drug Act and the Hepburn Act. Roosevelt is awarded the Nobel Peace Prize

1907 Half a million foreigners pass through the immigration center on Ellis Island

1908 William Howard Taft elected president. U.S. Supreme Court decision, *Muller v. Oregon*

1908–09 Roosevelt dispatches the "Great White Fleet" on worldwide tour

1911 Triangle Shirtwaist Company Fire. Before year's end, NY legislature establishes the Factory Investigating Commission

1912 Woodrow Wilson elected president. Roosevelt shot during the campaign. Massachusetts passes the first minimum wage law

1913 Congress passes the Sixteenth and Seventeenth Amendments. Federal Reserve Act established. President Taft intervenes in Honduras and Nicaragua

1914 The Panama Canal is completed. President Wilson invades Mexico, occupying Veracruz. World War I starts in Europe

1916 Wilson reelected president. Congress passes Federal Farm Loan Act, Adamson Act, Keating–Owen Act, Federal Highways Act, and Kern–McGillicuddy Act

1916–17 General Pershing leads punitive expedition in Mexico, but fails to capture Pancho Villa

1917 U.S. Supreme Court decision, *Bunting v. Oregon*

1918 End of World War I

1919 Eighteenth Amendment is ratified

1920 Nineteenth Amendment is ratified

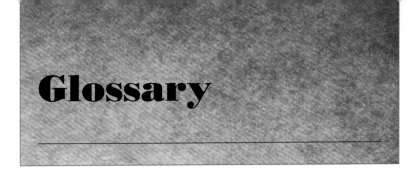

Glossary

anarchist A person who opposes all forms of organized government.

arbitration Solving a disagreement between two parties through the intervention of a third party.

Bessemer process A method of producing steel by applying blasts of hot air to molten iron to burn off carbon.

"big stick" diplomacy Theodore Roosevelt's aggressive manner of conducting foreign relations with the aim of increasing U.S. influence in the world.

capital Money invested to expand a business. This money could be used to purchase raw materials, pay workers, build premises, or cover shipping costs.

corporation A business that is owned by investors who purchase stock, thus becoming shareholders.

diplomacy The art of negotiation between different nations.

"dollar diplomacy" President Taft's policy of using economic means to reach diplomatic objectives.

expansionism Taking control of another nation's territory through political, economic, or military means; the policy was similar to imperialism as practiced in the 1890s.

foreign policy The diplomatic policies and position taken by a nation in its interaction with other nations, particularly to protect its own interests.

imperialism Establishing colonies and building empires.

initiative The right to initiate legislation, which allowed citizens to develop and vote on a law that their state legislature chose not to consider.

mass production Making lots of products fast and cheaply, usually in a factory.

monopoly A business that has total or almost complete control over an entire industry.

muckrakers Newspaper reporters and other writers who pointed out the social and political ills of the era of big business.

Mugwumps The most honest wing of the Republican party during the Gilded Age.

neutrality Refusal to take sides.

"open door" policy A policy giving all nations equal access to trade in China.

patronage The political practice of rewarding supporters by appointing them to non-elected, bureaucratic offices.

political machine Political insiders who offered patronage in exchange for political support. These political bosses were not elected, but manipulated the political process and had the power to hand out city contracts.

pooling agreement A method used by railroad companies to end competition. Several companies in a geographic area would agree to charge the same freight rates and were thus able to set their prices high.

populism A farm-based movement of the late 1800s that arose mainly in the Midwest and developed into an effort to battle big business and corrupt politics.

progressivism A political movement in the late 1800s and early 1900s whose goals were to increase democracy, correct social and economic ills, and curb the power of the trusts. Progressives also fought for honest government.

rebate A discount given secretly by the railroads to their largest customers.

recall Removing a public official from office, due to incompetence or failure to do the job.

referendum The opportunity for voters to decide on an issue that was previously rejected by a state's lawmakers.

Roosevelt Corollary A declaration made by President Theodore Roosevelt in 1904, which stated that the United States could intervene in any Latin American country that was weak or guilty of wrong doings.

secret ballot A ballot in which voters make their decisions in private and hence do not reveal who they vote for or how they vote on an issue.

socialism An economic system in which the production and distribution of goods are controlled by the government, rather than by private enterprise.

Stalwarts The most corrupt wing of the Republican Party during the Gilded Age.

stock Shares in a business. Stock is usually sold to investors, or stockholders, who buy in the hope of receiving a dividend, or a share of the profits.

sweatshop A factory or other workplace where employees work under poor conditions for low pay.

Teller Amendment The final clause of Congress's 1898 war declaration against Spain, which stated that the Cubans would govern themselves when peace was restored.

trust A group of corporations run by a single board of directors.

trust busting Seeking to prosecute or dissolve business trusts and break up large monopolies.

union An organization that seeks to improve wages and working conditions for people working in one particular trade or line of work.

vertical integration Control of all aspects of an industry, or of all the steps required to change raw materials into finished products.

yellow journalism Exaggerated or fabricated stories published in a newspaper.

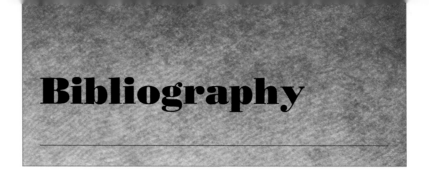

Bibliography

Athearn, Robert G. *The Progressive Era, 1901–1917*. New York: Time Incorporated, 1963.

Bilhartz, Terry. *Currents in American History: A Brief History of the United States: From 1861*. Armonk, NY: M. E. Sharpe, 2007.

Blow, Michael. *A Ship to Remember: The Maine and the Spanish–American War*. New York: William Morrow and Co., Inc., 1992.

Boller, Paul. *Presidential Campaigns from George Washington to George W. Bush*. NY: Oxford University Press, 2004.

Chernow, Ron. *The House of Morgan: An American Banking Dynasty and the Rise of Modern Finance*. New York: Grove Press, 2001.

Clanton, O. Gene. *A Common Humanity: Kansas Populism and the Battle for Justice and Equality, 1854–1903*. Manhattan, KS: Sunflower University Press, 2004.

Crunden, Robert. *Ministers of Reform: The Progressives' Achievement in American Civilization, 1889–1920*. Champaign: University of Illinois Press, 1985.

Cutler, Thomas. *A Sailor's History of the U.S. Navy*. Annapolis, MY: Naval Institute Press, 2004.

Evans, Harold. *The American Century*. New York: Alfred Knopf, 1998.

Halper, Sam, et al. *This Fabulous Century: Prelude, 1870–1900*. New York: Time-Life Books, 1970.

Heffner, Richard. *A Documentary History of the United States*. New York: Signet Books, 2002.

Hofstadter, Richard. *The American Political tradition and the Men Who Made It*. New York: Alfred A. Knopf, 1973.

Johnson, William Weber. *Heroic Mexico: The Violent Emergence of a Modern Nation*. Garden City, NY: Doubleday, 1968.

Josephson, Matthew. *The Robber Barons: The Classic Account of the Influential Capitalists Who Transformed America's Future*. New York: Harcourt, Brace and Company, 1934.

Keene, Jennifer D. *World War I*. Westport, CT: Greenwood Press, 2006.

LeFeber, Walter. *Inevitable Revolutions: The United States in Central America*. New York: W. W. Norton and Co, 1983.

Martin, James Kirby. *America and Its People*. New York: HarperCollins, 1993.

McCullough, David. *The Path Between the Seas: The Creation of the Panama Canal, 1870–1914*. New York: Simon and Schuster, 1977.

Roosevelt, Theodore. *The Rough Riders / An Autobiography*. New York: Library of America, 2004.

Salinger, Lawrence M. *Encyclopedia of White-Collar and Corporate Crime. Volume II*. Thousand Oaks, CA: Sage Publications, 2004.

Smith, Gene. *Until the Last Trumpet Sounds: The Life of General of the Armies John J. Pershing*. New York: John Wiley & Sons, Inc., 1998.

Snow, Richard F. "American Characters: Sockless Jerry Simpson." *American Heritage Magazine*. February 1978.
————. "Thank You, Private SNAFU." *American Heritage Magazine*. May/June 1995.

Tedlow, Richard S. *Giants of Enterprise: Seven Business Innovators and the Empires They Built*. New York: Collins, 2001.

Tindall, George Brown and David Emory Shi. *America, A Narrative History*. New York: W. W. Norton & Co., 1997.

Weinstein, Allen. *The Story of America: Freedom and Crisis From Settlement to Superpower*. New York: DK Publishing, Inc., 2002.

Weisberger, Bernard. *Reaching for Empire: 1890–1901*. New York: Time Incorporated, 1964.

Welsome, Eileen. *The General and the Jaguar: Pershing's Hunt for Pancho Villa, The True Story of Revolution and Revenge*. Lincoln, NE: Bison Books, 2007.

Further Resources

Burgan, Michael. *J. Pierpont Morgan: Industrialist and Financier*. Mankato, MN: Coughlan, 2006.

Cefrey, Holly. *The Sherman Antitrust Act: Getting Big Business Under Control*. New York: Rosen, 2004.

Collier, Christopher, and James Lincoln Collier. *Progressivism, the Great Depression and the New Deal, 1901–1941*. New York: Benchmark Books, 2001.

Edge, Laura. *Andrew Carnegie*. Minneapolis: Lerner, 2003.

Flagler, John J. *Labor Movement in the United States*. Minneapolis: Lerner, 1990.

Freedman, Russell. *Kids at Work: Lewis Hine and the Crusade Against Child Labor*. New York: Clarion Books, 1994.

Link, Arthur Stanley. *Progressivism*. Wheeling, IL: Davidson, Harlan, 1983.

McNeese, Tim. *John J. Pershing*. Philadelphia: Chelsea House Publishers, 2004.

————. *The Labor Movement: Unionizing America*. New York: Chelsea House Publishers, 2008.

————. *The Progressive Movement: Advocating Social Change*. New York: Chelsea House Publishers, 2008.

————. *Remember the Maine: The Spanish–American War Begins*. Greensboro, NC: Morgan Reynolds Publishers, Inc., 2002.

Parker, Lewis K. *J. Pierpont Morgan and Wall Street*. New York: Rosen, 2003.

————. *John D. Rockefeller and the Oil Industry*. New York: Rosen, 2003.

Sakany, Lois. *Platforms and Policies of America's Reform Politicians*. New York: Rosen Publishing Group, 2004.

Segall, Grant. *John D. Rockefeller: Anointed with Oil.* New York: Oxford University Press, 2001.

White, Anne Terry. *Eugene Debs: American Socialist.* Chicago: Chicago Review Press, 1974.

Web sites

The Battleship *Maine:*
   http://www.arlingtoncemetery.com/ussmaine.htm
   http://www.history.navy.mil/photos/events/spanam/events/
      maineskg.htm

Big Business and the Robber Barons:
   http://www.spartacus.schoolnet.co.uk/USAmorgan.htm
   http://www.biographyshelf.com/andrew_carnegie_
      biography.html
   http://history.sandiego.edu/gen/soc/robber-barons.html
   http://bellevuelinux.org/sherman.html
   http://www.biographyshelf.com/thomas_edison_
      biography.html
   http://www.socialstudieshelp.com/Lesson_44_Notes.htm

Gilded Age Politics:
   http://www.sagehistory.net/gildedage/GildedAPolitics.htm
   http://historymatters.gmu.edu/d/5354/

Labor Movement:
   http://www.historyplace.com/unitedstates/childlabor/
      index.html
   http://www.u-s-history.com/pages/h1678.html
   http://www.phoenixmasonry.org/masonicmuseum/
      fraternalism/knights_of_labor.htm

Progressivism:
   http://www.historyteacher.net/USProjects/USQuizzes/
      Progressivism1.htm

Spanish–American War:
   http://www.spanamwar.com/

Picture Credits

Index

About the Author

Tim McNeese is associate professor of history at York College in York, Nebraska. Professor McNeese holds degrees from York College, Harding University, and Missouri State University. He has published more than 100 books and educational materials. His writing has earned him a citation in the library reference work, *Contemporary Authors* and multiple citations in *Best Books for Young Teen Readers*. In 2006, Tim appeared on the History Channel program, *Risk Takers, History Makers: John Wesley Powell and the Grand Canyon*. He was been a faculty member at the Tony Hillerman Writers Conference in Albuquerque. His wife, Beverly is assistant professor of English at York College. They have two married children, Noah and Summer, and three grandchildren—Ethan, Adrianna, and Finn William. Tim and Bev have sponsored college study trips on the Lewis and Clark Trail and to the American Southwest. You may contact Professor McNeese at tdmcneese@york.edu.

About the Consultant

Richard Jensen is Research Professor at Montana State University, Billings. He has published 11 books on a wide range of topics in American political, social, military, and economic history, as well as computer methods. After taking a Ph.D. at Yale in 1966, he taught at numerous universities, including Washington, Michigan, Harvard, Illinois-Chicago, West Point, and Moscow State University in Russia.